California Legal Research

CAROLINA ACADEMIC PRESS
LEGAL RESEARCH SERIES

Suzanne E. Rowe, Series Editor

꙳

Arizona, Second Edition—Tamara S. Herrera

Arkansas—Coleen M. Barger

California, Second Edition—Hether C. Macfarlane, Aimee Dudovitz &
Suzanne E. Rowe

Colorado—Robert Michael Linz

Connecticut—Jessica G. Hynes

Federal—Mary Garvey Algero, Spencer L. Simons, Suzanne E. Rowe,
Scott Childs & Sarah E. Ricks

Florida, Third Edition, Revised Printing—Barbara J. Busharis
& Suzanne E. Rowe

Georgia—Nancy P. Johnson, Elizabeth G. Adelman & Nancy J. Adams

Idaho—Tenielle Fordyce-Ruff & Suzanne E. Rowe

Illinois, Second Edition—Mark E. Wojcik

Iowa—John D. Edwards, M. Sara Lowe, Karen L. Wallace
& Melissa H. Weresh

Kansas—Joseph A. Custer & Christopher L. Steadham

Kentucky—William A. Hilyerd, Kurt X. Metzmeier & David J. Ensign

Louisiana, Second Edition—Mary Garvey Algero

Massachusetts—E. Joan Blum

Michigan, Second Edition—Pamela Lysaght & Cristina D. Lockwood

Minnesota—Suzanne Thorpe

Missouri, Second Edition—Wanda M. Temm & Julie M. Cheslik

New York, Second Edition—Elizabeth G. Adelman, Theodora Belniak
& Suzanne E. Rowe

North Carolina—Scott Childs

Ohio—Katherine L. Hall & Sara Sampson

Oklahoma—Darin K. Fox, Darla W. Jackson & Courtney L. Selby

Oregon, Second Edition, Revised Printing—Suzanne E. Rowe

Pennsylvania—Barbara J. Busharis & Bonny L. Tavares

Tennessee—Sibyl Marshall & Carol McCrehan Parker

Texas, Revised Printing—Spencer L. Simons

Washington, Second Edition—Julie Heintz-Cho, Tom Cobb
& Mary A. Hotchkiss

West Virginia—Hollee Schwartz Temple

Wisconsin—Patricia Cervenka & Leslie Behroozi

Wyoming—Debora Person & Tawnya Plumb

꙳

California Legal Research

Second Edition

Hether C. Macfarlane

Aimee Dudovitz

Suzanne E. Rowe

Suzanne E. Rowe, Series Editor

CAROLINA ACADEMIC PRESS

Durham, North Carolina

Library of Congress Cataloging-in-Publication Data

Macfarlane, Hether C.
California legal research / Hether C. Macfarlane, Aimee Dudovitz, Suzanne E. Rowe. -- Second Edition.
pages cm
Includes bibliographical references and index.
ISBN 978-1-61163-382-5 (alk. paper)
1. Legal research--California. I. Dudovitz, Aimee. II. Rowe, Suzanne E., 1961- III. Title.

KFC74.M33 2013
340.072'0794--dc23

2013019694

CAROLINA ACADEMIC PRESS
700 Kent Street
Durham, North Carolina 27701
Telephone (919) 489-7486
Fax (919) 493-5668
www.cap-press.com

Printed in the United States of America.

Dedicated

to Stephen and Ellen
H.C.M.

to Joshua and Jeffrey
A.D.

and to Didi Alfred
S.E.R.

Summary of Contents

Contents

List of Tables, Figures, and Appendices

Tables

Figures

Appendices

Series Note

The Legal Research Series published by Carolina Academic Press includes titles from states around the country as well as a separate text on federal legal research. The goal of each book is to provide law students, practitioners, paralegals, college students, laypeople, and librarians with the essential elements of legal research in each jurisdiction. Unlike more bibliographic texts, the Legal Research Series books seek to explain concisely both the sources of legal research and the process for conducting legal research effectively.

Preface to the Second Edition

The second edition of *California Legal Research* reflects the great changes seen in legal research in the past few years. Fewer libraries house print sources, and more researchers rely on online sources. Lexis.com and Westlaw Classic are being replaced by Lexis Advance and WestlawNext. The text remains true to the goal of the first edition: to explain both the sources and the process for researching California law.

In updating the text, we have avoided making changes that were not essential, and we expect the second edition to feel familiar to readers of the first edition. Some of the more important changes are outlined below:

Chapter 1 diminishes the distinction between print and online research, recognizing the growing dominance of online resources. Given that online research techniques work similarly for cases, statutes, administrative regulations, and other sources, Chapter 1 presents a revised research outline that includes under one step searching for all primary authorities. These authorities are still explained in separate chapters later in the book.

Chapter 2 continues its focus on Lexis and Westlaw products. It now covers both the classic versions and the next generation versions of each service. We use "Lexis" and "Westlaw" as umbrella terms to cover both versions. To be specific, Lexis.com and Lexis Advance designate the classic and new products provided by Lexis, while Westlaw Classic and WestlawNext designate the products provided by Westlaw. Chapter 2 covers other online products in a brief section at the end. We chose to continue focusing on Lexis and Westlaw products as they are most widely used and most relevant to California-specific research.

In this edition, Chapter 3 explains judicial opinions, while Chapter 4 covers researching them. A single chapter in the first edition covered both an introduction to judicial opinions and how to research them.

Chapter 9 (formerly Chapter 8) no longer has an appendix explaining Shepardizing in print, as fewer libraries maintain current volumes. The chapter has been slightly reorganized: general information about citator symbols, the importance of reading citing references, and the utility of narrowing search results has been moved to the beginning of the chapter because those topics apply to research with all citators.

Chapter 10 (formerly Chapter 9), on secondary sources, no longer focuses primarily on print research. In addition, it presents Witkin alone, not with treatises, recognizing its unique importance to California research. This chapter expands the discussion of Rutter Group materials and jury instructions, while decreasing the attention given to continuing legal education materials, consistent with California practice. It no longer has a separate section on mini-libraries.

We try throughout to present a balanced coverage of the products of Lexis and Westlaw. For example, in some chapters we tend to discuss Lexis first while in other chapters Westlaw gets the first nod.

With this edition, we welcome a new co-author, Aimee Dudovitz, of Loyola Law School—Los Angeles. Professor Dudovitz brought particular expertise to the chapter on legislative history, and she was primarily responsible for updating that chapter as well as the chapter on administrative law. Professor Macfarlane was responsible for updating the two chapters on cases as well as chapters on statutes and constitutions. Professor Rowe updated the remaining chapters, though again the work on the book was a collaborative effort. Some portions of this book are drawn from *Oregon Legal Research*, which has served as a guide for a number of books in the Legal Research Series.

Hether C. Macfarlane
Aimee Dudovitz
Suzanne E. Rowe

California Legal Research

Chapter 1

The Research Process and Legal Analysis

I. California Legal Research

The fundamentals of legal research are the same in every American jurisdiction, though the details vary. While some variations are minor, others require specialized knowledge of the resources available and the analytical framework in which those resources are used. This book focuses on the resources and analysis required to be thorough and effective in researching California law. It supplements this focus with brief explanations of federal research and research into the law of other states, both to introduce other resources and to highlight some of the variations.

II. The Intersection of Legal Research and Legal Analysis

The basic process of legal research is often quite simple. For most online research, you will search particular websites or sources using words likely to appear in the text of relevant documents. For most print resources, you will begin with an index, find entries that appear relevant, read those sections of the text, and then find out whether more recent information is available.

Legal analysis is interwoven throughout this process, raising challenging questions. How will you choose the search terms most likely to lead to the documents you need? When you read the text of a document, how will you determine whether it is relevant to your client's situation? How will you learn whether more recent material changed the law or applied it in a new situation? The answer to each of these questions requires legal analysis. This intersection of research and analysis can make legal research very difficult, especially for the novice. While this book's focus is legal research, it also includes the fundamental aspects of legal analysis required to conduct research competently.

III. Types of Legal Authority

The goal of legal research is to find constitutional provisions, statutes, administrative rules, and judicial opinions that control a client's situation. In other words, you are searching for primary, mandatory authority.

Law is often divided along two lines. The first line distinguishes primary authority from secondary authority. *Primary authority* is law produced by government bodies with law-making power. Legislatures write statutes, courts write judicial opinions, and administrative agencies write regulations. *Secondary authority* includes all other legal sources, such as treatises, law review articles, legal encyclopedias, and blogs. They may be written by attorneys, judges, and law professors; by the editorial staff of publishing companies; or by law students. These secondary sources are designed to aid researchers in understanding the law and locating primary authority.

Another division is made between mandatory and persuasive authority. *Mandatory authority* is binding on the court that would decide a conflict if the situation were litigated. In a question of California law, mandatory authority includes California's constitution, statutes enacted by the California Legislature, California administrative rules, and opinions of the Supreme Court of California.[1] *Persua-*

---

1. An opinion from the California Court of Appeal is binding on trial courts throughout California if the Supreme Court of California has not addressed a particular topic. *See Auto Equity Sales, Inc. v. Super. Ct. of Santa*

sive authority is not binding, but may be followed if relevant and well reasoned. Authority may be merely persuasive if it is from a different jurisdiction or if it is not produced by a law-making body. In a question of California law, examples of persuasive authority would include a similar Washington statute, an opinion of an Oregon state court, and a law review article. Notice in Table 1-1 that persuasive authority may be either primary or secondary authority, while mandatory authority is always primary.

Table 1-1. Examples of Authority in California Research

	Mandatory Authority	Persuasive Authority
Primary Authority	California statutes California Supreme Court cases California regulations	Washington statutes Oregon Supreme Court cases Nevada regulations
Secondary Authority	—	Law review articles Legal encyclopedias Treatises Restatements

Within primary, mandatory authority, there is an interlocking hierarchy of law involving constitutions, statutes, administrative rules, and judicial opinions. The state's constitution is the supreme law of that state. Statutes come next in the hierarchy, followed by administrative rules. Judicial opinions interpret the statutes and rules; moreover, a judicial opinion may hold that a statute violates the constitution or that a rule oversteps its bounds. In California, a court can "reform" or rewrite a state statute to avoid invalidating it on specific constitutional grounds when the intention of the legislature or the electorate is clear.[2] If there is no constitutional provision, statute, or

---

Clara Co., 57 Cal. 2d 450, 455–56 (1962). If the districts conflict, the trial courts are free to choose among the conflicting decisions. *See id.* at 456.

2. *Kopp v. Fair Political Practices Comm'n*, 11 Cal. 4th 607, 615 (1995).

administrative rule on point, the issue will be controlled by *common law,* also called judge-made law.[3]

IV. Overview of the Research Process

Conducting effective legal research means following a process. This process leads to the authority that controls a legal issue as well as to commentary that may help you analyze new and complex legal matters. The outline in Table 1-2 presents the basic research process.

Table 1-2. Overview of the Research Process

1. **Prepare**
   Gather facts, identify the research issue, determine the relevant jurisdiction, and list research terms.

2. **Learn**
   Consult secondary sources and practice aids, including treatises, legal encyclopedias, and law review articles. These will provide context and background on your issue and might point to primary authority.

3. **Search**
   Look for enacted law in the relevant jurisdiction, including constitutional provisions, statutes, and administrative regulations. Gather citations to relevant cases.

4. **Read**
   Take time throughout your research to read carefully the authorities you are locating.

5. **Update**
   Use citators to update or "Shepardize" your legal authorities to ensure they are current and to find additional relevant authorities.

6. **Finish**
   In general, your research is complete when there are no holes remaining in your analysis and when searches in different sources produce the same set of authorities.

---

3. Common law is derived from judicial decisions, rather than statutes or constitutions. *Black's Law Dictionary* 313 (Bryan A. Garner ed., 9th ed., West 2009).

A. Prepare to Research

Before beginning to research, collect the information you have available about the project. Gather facts from client interviews, colleagues working with you on the project, documents in the client file, and other sources. At the same time, gather practical facts about your project, including the deadline and the research sources at your disposal. Also, identify the legal issue you need to research. If you are working for a supervisor, that person will likely tell you what the issue is. When you are working on your own, your first research might be aimed at determining the legal issues that might exist. Next, be sure that you know the relevant jurisdiction. Your project might be governed by international law, federal law, state law, local law, or tribal law, or by a combination of those.

Your last preparatory step is listing research terms. Legal research—whether online or in print—often begins with a list of words that are relevant to the topic of the research project. To ensure thorough research, you will need a comprehensive list of words, terms, and phrases that may lead to law on point. These may be legal terms or common words that describe the client's situation.

Organized brainstorming is the best way to compile a comprehensive list of research terms. Some researchers ask the journalistic questions: Who? What? How? Why? When? Where? Others use a mnemonic device like TARPP, which stands for Things, Actions, Remedies, People, and Places. Whether you use one of these suggestions or develop your own method, generate a broad range of research terms regarding the facts, issues, and desired solutions of your client's situation. Include in the list both specific and general words. Try to think of synonyms and antonyms for each term, especially when working with print sources or less sophisticated online search engines. Using a legal dictionary or thesaurus—often provided by online services—may help to generate additional terms.

As an example, assume a client has suffered nightmares and anxiety attacks after the following scene at a restaurant in San Diego. He and his wife were having lunch at an outside table near the street. The man went inside to the restroom, and as he returned to the table he heard a car crash. He saw a table umbrella fall and felt pieces of glass from a shattered mirror. A car had jumped the curb and hit his wife. Although she eventually recovered from her serious injuries, he has continued to suffer serious emotional symptoms. Your supervisor asks you to research whether the client has a claim for negligent infliction of emotion distress against the driver, even though the client was merely an observer or bystander to the accident. You know that California is the relevant jurisdiction. Table 1-3 provides examples of research terms you might use to begin work on this project.

Table 1-3. Generating Research Terms
Journalistic Approach

Who:	Driver, spouse, husband, bystander
What:	Car accident, lingering symptoms, anxiety, nightmares
How:	Being near accident that injured spouse
Why:	Reckless driving, witnessing accident
When:	Daytime, lunch hour
Where:	Restaurant, San Diego, street side, near sidewalk

B. Learn About the Topic

Most lawyers begin researching an unfamiliar area of law by turning to secondary sources. These sources include books written by practicing attorneys, law review articles, and encyclopedia entries. They also include websites and blogs. Secondary sources are helpful because they summarize, explain, and sometimes analyze the law. Often a secondary source will be easier to understand than a statute or a judicial opinion. Secondary sources are also helpful because they contain references to relevant statutes, regulations, cases, and other legal material.

C. Search for Primary Authority

1. Finding Constitutional Provisions and Statutes

California's constitution is the highest legal authority on state matters. It begins with fundamental rights that are similar to those ensured by the federal constitution. Article I of the California Constitution provides, "All people are by nature free and independent and have inalienable rights. Among these are enjoying and defending life and liberty, acquiring, possessing, and protecting property, and pursuing and obtaining safety, happiness, and privacy." But the state constitution is not identical to the federal constitution, and it contains provisions that are more statutory in nature. For example, Article 10B of the California Constitution is known as the Marine Resources Protection Act of 1990; it prohibits the use of gill nets and trammel nets in certain zones.

The California Legislature has enacted statutes on many topics. Statutes are organized by subject matter in twenty-nine codes ranging from "Civil Procedure" to "Labor" to "Revenue and Taxation." A list of the twenty-nine codes is provided in Chapter 6 at Table 6-2. An example of a single statute is section 451 of the Penal Code, which sets the penalties for arson (see Figure 6-2).

2. Researching Administrative Law

California has over 200 state regulatory agencies. These agencies issue regulations on matters ranging from drivers' licenses to environmental protection. The regulations are codified in twenty-eight titles in the California Code of Regulations; these are listed in Table 8-2 in Chapter 8. An example of a regulation is provided in Figure 8-2. Agencies also decide disputes regarding the agencies' regulations. Although only a few law school courses address administrative law, it is a significant area of law and must be considered in a complete research process.

3. Researching Judicial Opinions

Courts write judicial opinions to explain their decisions in the cases that come before them. Some opinions are based on statutory law; the courts in these cases apply the statutory requirements to the facts of the parties before them. Other opinions are based on administrative law; most often, these cases are appeals from decisions by administrative agencies. When no statute or administrative rule controls, judicial opinions are based on the common law.

Judicial opinions are published in rough chronological order in books called *reporters*. There are multiple reporters for California opinions, which will be covered in Chapter 3. Even when you read cases online, their citations are most often to print reporters; thus, understanding reporters is important even when researching using exclusively online sources. The first page of a California case is reproduced in Figure 3-1. Appendices to Chapter 3 show the first screen of the same case as seen on WestlawNext and Lexis Advance, two premier sources for online legal research.

Cases relevant to your project may be discussed in secondary sources or listed alongside relevant statutes. You can further research case law with topical indexes or by using search engines that scan the full text of cases in a database.

D. Read Authorities Carefully

One of the most important and time-consuming aspects of legal research is reading the authorities that you locate. While online services are making it increasingly easy to read, highlight, and save documents on their websites, do not underestimate the value of printing key authorities and reading them repeatedly in hard copy.

E. Update with Citators

After finding statutes, cases, and other authorities that address a research topic, you must ensure that these authorities represent the current law. This step is performed using *citators*. The process of using citators to ensure that authorities are still respected is called updating. For example, a citator will produce a list of authorities that have mentioned a case you have decided is relevant, along with indications of whether the authorities agreed with the case or not. (Several samples of citator lists appear in Chapter 9.) By reviewing the list, you can learn whether that case has been reversed, overruled, distinguished, or followed extensively.

Because citators provide lists of authorities, they are also effective finding tools. Entering the citation for one relevant case can quickly produce a list of other cases that may be relevant because they relied on a case you know is relevant.

F. Finish the Research

The goal of research is to solve a client's problem. If you immediately find a primary authority that perfectly answers the client's question, your research may be over. Most research projects, however, do not have a clear answer. You will have to collect bits and pieces of answers to construct a solution that meets your client's goals. When there is no clear answer, it can be difficult to know when to stop researching. There are two checkpoints for knowing that research is nearing an end.

First, make an outline of your answer to the client's problems. When there are no analytical holes in the outline, you are likely finished researching. Second, in reviewing secondary sources, statutes, administrative law, and judicial opinions, and then updating relevant authorities, it is likely that you will begin to see the same authorities appear repeatedly. No longer finding new authorities is an excellent sign that your research has been thorough and you should stop looking for additional authorities.

G. Modify the Process

The basic research process should be customized for each research project. Consider whether you need to follow all six steps, and if so, in what order. If you are unfamiliar with an area of law, you should follow each step of the process in the order indicated. Beginning with secondary sources will provide both context for the issues you must research and citations to relevant primary authority. As you gain experience in researching legal questions, you may choose to modify the process. For example, if you know that a situation is controlled by a statute, you may choose to begin with that step. Or if you know of a case that is on point, you may decide to update it immediately to find additional cases on the same point. Research strategies are discussed in more detail in Chapter 11.

V. Researching the Law—Organization of This Text

Chapter 2 of this book explains fundamental search techniques for legal research. The remaining chapters explain in depth how to research different legal resources.[4] Chapter 3 covers the California court system and judicial opinions, while Chapter 4 explains how to find judicial opinions in a variety of online and print sources. Case research is covered first because most legal research will include finding and reading cases, even when other primary authority is on point. Chapter 5 addresses the California Constitution, which is the highest legal authority in the state. Chapter 6 describes researching statutes, and Chapter 7 discusses legislative history research. Chapter 8 addresses administrative law.

After this focus on primary authority, Chapter 9 explains how to update legal authority using citators like Shepard's and KeyCite. Chapter 10 covers secondary sources, the frequent starting point for research in an unfamiliar area of law. The discussion of secondary sources is delayed to emphasize their subordinate position relative to primary authority. Chapter 11 discusses research strategies as well as how to organize your research. You may prefer to skim that chapter now and refer to it frequently, even though a number of references in it will not become clear until you have read the intervening chapters.

Chapter 12 provides an overview of the conventions lawyers follow in citing legal authority in their documents. In addition to dis-

---

4. Law students using this book in a research class will most likely cover the chapters in a different order, reflecting the research strategies needed to complement their other coursework.

cussing California citations under the *California Style Manual*,[5] this chapter introduces the two national citation manuals, the *ALWD Citation Manual: A Professional System of Citation*[6] and *The Bluebook: A Uniform System of Citation*.[7]

---

5. Edward W. Jessen, *California Style Manual* (4th ed., West 2000) ("*CSM*").

6. ALWD & Darby Dickerson, *ALWD Citation Manual: A Professional System of Citation* (4th ed., Aspen Publishers 2010) ("*ALWD Manual*"). While most citations in this book conform to the *ALWD Manual*, case citations are to official California reporters, reflecting the common practice among California lawyers.

7. *The Bluebook: A Uniform System of Citation* (The Columbia Law Review et al. eds., 19th ed., The Harvard Law Review Ass'n 2010) ("*Bluebook*").

Chapter 2

Legal Research Techniques

Legal research uses print sources, government and law library websites, and online providers like Lexis and Westlaw. While each resource is slightly different, some basic research techniques are shared in common. This chapter covers the basic techniques for using print and online legal resources. Researchers experienced in either print or online resources will find this chapter a helpful review. Those with less experience in one type of resource will need to consider these techniques carefully, as later chapters assume familiarity with them.

This chapter begins with print research techniques because many online services are still based on print sources. The chapter focuses primarily on the online service providers Lexis and Westlaw because they remain the leaders in California legal research. Other online services are introduced at the end of the chapter.

I. Print Research Techniques

Today, fewer researchers approach legal problems with a firm foundation in print research techniques. In large part, this is because so much information is available online, which has decreased the demand for print sources among students and professionals. In legal research, however, not all material is available online. Even when sources are available both online and in print, print sources are sometimes more efficient to use. The efficiency may be simply because the sources are free in a library. More often, the efficiency results from the way the resources are organized.

A. Finding a Legal Source by Citation

Retrieving a document in a print source is easy when you have its citation. Simply find the relevant book and turn to the portion indicated by the citation. The citation may be to a particular volume and page (e.g., for a judicial opinion), a title and section (e.g., for a statute), or a paragraph or section number (e.g., a legal encyclopedia). Example citations are listed below.

Example judicial opinion:	*People v. Davis*, 18 Cal. 4th 712 (1998).
Example statute:	Cal. Penal Code Ann. §451 (West 2010).
Example encyclopedia:	18A Cal. Jur. 3d *Criminal Law: Crimes Against Property* §39 (2009).

B. Table-of-Contents Searching

Most print sources begin with a table of contents. One way to search these sources is to skim the table of contents for your research terms. The table of contents will refer to relevant pages, section numbers, or paragraph numbers, depending on how that source is organized.

Because a table of contents lists the headings used in that volume, it provides an analytical overview of the topics covered. Skimming the table of contents of an encyclopedia can show how lawyers typically organize concepts in a particular area of law. Reviewing a table of contents for a statutory provision can provide context for the analysis of a single statute. Thus, you can use the table of contents both to get an overview of the law and to find specific portions of the volume that may contain helpful information.

C. Topic Searching with a Print Index

The index—an alphabetical listing of topics included in a book or series of books—is another frequent starting point in print resources. Using the research terms you generated based on the client's problem, search the index for references to particular pages or sections of the volume. Often, it is wise to spend several minutes in the index looking for a number of research terms. This technique ensures that you begin your research in the most helpful part of the volume, not just the part you encountered first. It is common for an index to contain cross-references to other entries. Take a few moments to learn the cross-reference signals of a new book, as they vary among resources.

In multi-volume series, the index is likely to be located in the last volume. Separate indexes may be provided for each volume or for each legal topic. In a digest,[1] for example, the "Analysis" outline at the beginning of a topic can provide context for the concepts covered and suggest particular portions of the topic that may lead to relevant cases.

D. Pocket Parts and Supplements

Many print sources are updated using *pocket parts*. These are extra pages sent by the publisher to be inserted in the back cover of a particular volume. Pocket parts often contain the most recent material available in print, so it is important to check any volume used in research to see whether it has a pocket part. If a pocket part becomes too large to fit in the back of a volume, it will be published as a softbound supplement and shelved next to the volume. Eventually, the publisher will print a new version of the bound volume and will incorporate the material from the pocket part and supplements into that volume.

In addition to updates to single volumes, a softbound supplement may exist for an entire series of books. This supplement will likely be shelved at the end of the series. It will contain the most up-to-date information available in print.

---

1. Digests are a form of index for case reporters; the digests referenced in this paragraph are the traditional, print versions, though digests are also available online. Digests are covered in Chapter 4.

II. Online Research Techniques with Lexis and Westlaw

Lawyers often find online research necessary for conducting efficient and cost-effective legal research. While the most advanced online services provide Google-like searching capacity, other online sources require a high level of precision in deciding where to search and in constructing searches. Regardless of the service used, online searching can produce large numbers of results that you must sift through to locate relevant documents. This part of the chapter begins with basic information for conducting legal research online. The chapter then delves into more advanced search techniques, focusing on Lexis and Westlaw services.

Table 2-1. Selected Government Websites for California Primary Authority

Type of Authority	Web Address
California Constitution	www.leginfo.ca.gov/const.html
California Statutes	www.leginfo.ca.gov/statute.html
California Regulations	www.oal.ca.gov (click on "California Code of Regulations")
California Appellate Opinions	www.courts.ca.gov/opinions.htm

Web addresses for California primary authority are listed in Table 2-1. The addresses for some commercial and university sites are listed in Table 2-2. Note that two addresses are given for the Lexis and Westlaw services. Lexis.com is the traditional service provided by Lexis-Nexis, while Lexis Advance is the new and still expanding product. Similarly, Westlaw Classic is the traditional service, and WestlawNext is the next generation service with Google-like search capacity. Other commercial, fee-based sites—including Bloomberg, Loislaw, Versus-Law—are addressed briefly at the end of this chapter. In addition to these resources, many legal researchers use "gateway" sites that link to a variety of online resources. Two university-provided gateway sites, Cornell University Law School's Legal Information Institute and Washburn University School of Law's WashLaw, are also included in Table 2-2.

Table 2-2. Commercial and Gateway Sites

Service/Provider	Web Address
Bloomberg	bloomberglaw.com
FindLaw	www.findlaw.com
Lexis.com	www.lexis.com
Lexis Advance	advance.lexis.com
Loislaw	estore.loislaw.com
VersusLaw	www.versuslaw.com
Westlaw Classic	web2.westlaw.com
WestlawNext	westlawnext.com
Gateway Sites	
Cornell University Law School's Legal Information Institute	www.law.cornell.edu
Washburn University School of Law's WashLaw	www.washlaw.edu

If the information you need is available for free on one of the government or university sites, think carefully before using a costly commercial provider. Sometimes a commercial provider's extensive database or sophisticated search engine will make the cost worthwhile, but you need to consider the costs and efficiencies involved in every search.

A. Finding a Legal Source by Citation

When working online, retrieving a document is as simple as typing the citation into a designated box on the proper screen. Note that online services typically use the print citation to identify particular documents. In other words, to retrieve a case from Lexis Advance, you will enter the volume and page of the print reporter. Many online providers list accepted citation formats, which vary from one online site to another.

Figure 2-1. Table-of-Contents Searching on WestlawNext

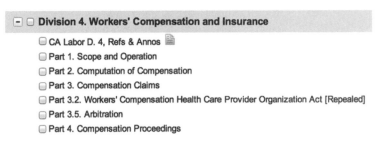

Source: Reprinted with permission of Thomson Reuters.

B. Table-of-Contents Searching

An increasing number of online sources provide tables of contents. As in print research, the advantages of skimming an online table of contents are (1) seeing how various issues and topics are related in that area of law, and (2) finding relevant portions of the document or database. An online table of contents works just like a table of contents in print, except that often the initial page will list only major headings. Subheadings may be accessed by clicking a symbol next to one of the headings; the symbol might be a "plus" or a triangle. On some services, you can either click on the name of a major heading, or check a box and click "Search" to access the table of contents.

For example, in a dispute over whether an injury that occurred at work is covered by California's workers' compensation laws, you could open the table of contents for California statutes on WestlawNext. It is available under "State Materials": click on "California" and then "California Statutes and Court Rules." Click on the heading "Labor" and scan the list until you find the "Labor Code." Clicking on the "+" symbol before that code would bring up the major divisions of that code, including "Division 4. Workers' Compensation and Insurance." Subsequent clicks lead to the division's parts, then chapters, and finally individual statutes. See Figure 2-1. It is possible to conduct the same type of search on the state website. See Figure 2-2.

Figure 2-2. Table-of-Contents Searching on California Legislative Site

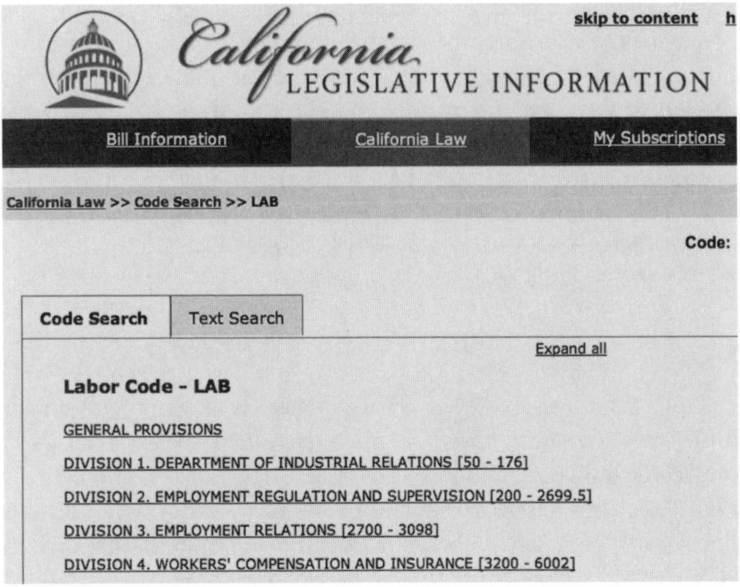

Source: California Legislature information, at http://leginfo.legislature.ca.gov/faces/codes.
xhtml (click on "Labor").

C. Natural-Language Searching

Natural-language search engines allow searches that use a simple question, phrase, or word. These search engines are designed to produce a list of results and to rank the value of the results. A natural-language search for the project in Chapter 1, for a researcher who does not know the cause of action, is "sue driver who injured wife causing husband emotional trauma." On WestlawNext, this search produces an excellent list of authorities. On less advanced services, including Westlaw Classic, natural-language searching might produce only limited results, so caution is advised.

1. Natural-Language Searching on Lexis Advance and WestlawNext

Lexis Advance and WestlawNext have sophisticated search engines that are designed for natural-language searching. With each of these services, you type search terms into a general search bar. You can limit the types of documents you retrieve (e.g., by jurisdiction or by type of law) before searching. You can then limit the search results by using filters. An added benefit of Lexis Advance and WestlawNext is that their algorithms look for not only the exact terms in your search but also related terms. For example, in researching "negligent infliction of emotion distress," a cause of action related to the project in Chapter 1, you could enter "NIED" and WestlawNext would return cases that included not only that abbreviation but also the full term "negligent infliction of emotional distress."

a. Lexis Advance

On Lexis Advance, the search bar appears at the top of any screen under the "Research" tab. Enter your terms, then select from three pre-search limitation tabs just under the search bar. A tab for content type allows you to select primary or secondary authorities, litigation documents, or news and business documents. A tab for jurisdiction allows you to select state or federal jurisdictions for searching. A third tab for practice areas and topics lets you limit the search to documents addressing certain legal subjects. Click "Search" to the right of the search bar to run the search within the limits selected. See Figure 2-3 for an example.

The search results will appear with a line of links along the top of the page. These links allow you to manipulate the results of your search so that you see just the material you want. The default link is a "Snapshot" that gives the top few documents under key categories including cases, statutes, secondary materials, forms, etc. To see all of the cases your search retrieved, click on the "Cases" link. This link will display each case by name, along with a brief excerpt showing how your search terms appear in the case.

Searches can return dozens if not hundreds of results. To allow you to find the most relevant authorities, Lexis Advance provides tools for narrowing the results. These tools are available along the left margin after clicking on the link for cases, statutes, or other document type, and the tools for narrowing vary by document type. For example, you can narrow cases by additional search terms, by court, by date, by

Figure 2-3. Searching on Lexis Advance

practice areas, by the attorneys or law firms involved, by the judges who heard the cases, etc. As a comparison, results under the legislation link can be narrowed by content type (e.g., legislative history, municipal code, or statute), by source (i.e., the publication), by practice area, and by keyword.

b. WestlawNext

Natural-language searching with WestlawNext is similar. The search bar appears at the top of the home page, with a tab for selecting the jurisdiction just to the right. Simply type in your search terms, select a jurisdiction, and click "Search."

The default screen for search results is called "Overview"; it provides a few of the cases, statutes, secondary sources, and other documents that West's search engine determines are most valuable for your search. In the left margin, you can view all of the results for any document type.

WestlawNext also provides filters so that you can refine your search. The filters vary depending on the type of document you are viewing. Under "Cases," the left margin provides filters for limiting

Figure 2-4. Filters on WestlawNext

search results by term, jurisdiction, date, topic, judge, attorney, etc. See Figure 2-4.

2. Natural-Language Searching with Other Services

Especially with the less advanced search engines, natural language is not a comprehensive way to search. Many researchers use it as an effective way to begin searching. Once they find a case that is on point, however, they refine their search using terms-and-connectors techniques that are explained later in this chapter or digests, which are explained in Chapter 4.

One of the difficulties of natural-language searching is that it can produce lists of documents that are not very relevant to your research. This result may mean that no better matches exist or that the search was not crafted well enough. When conducting the search on the Internet, poor results may mean that the particular search engine did not scan the portion of the Internet that contains the needed documents. On Lexis.com and Westlaw Classic, the natural-language programs are set to retrieve a particular number of results. Often that number is 20 or 100, though you can change the default. The fact that the computer returned 100 documents does not mean that those 100 documents are all relevant. One more caveat is important. On general purpose sites like Google, some hits appear first in result lists simply because sponsors pay for this privilege. Sometimes the best hit from your perspective will be the search engine's fifteenth result, so skimming through the results is always very important.

D. Terms-and-Connectors Searching

One of the most common techniques for searching online is with "terms and connectors." The following discussion addresses searching with terms and connectors on Lexis.com and Westlaw Classic, where this technique often produces better results than natural-language searching. (Although Lexis Advance and WestlawNext are designed so that you do not have to use term and connectors, the option remains available. On Lexis Advance, use "Search Tips" and "Connectors." In WestlawNext, you can either type a terms-and-connectors search into the general search bar or go to the "Advanced" page.)

Terms-and-connectors searches use connecting symbols to dictate where search terms should be in relation to each other in the documents retrieved. An outline of the steps to constructing an effective search is provided in Table 2-3.

Table 2-3. Outline for Constructing
Terms-and-Connectors Searches

---

1. Generate search terms, then modify them with expanders
   and placeholders.
2. Add connectors.
3. Choose the appropriate sources or databases to search.
4. Use relevant segments or fields to restrict the search by date,
   court, judge, or other option.
5. Refine the search based on the results.

---

1. Generate Search Terms

Generate a comprehensive list of search terms, following the suggestions in Chapter 1. This step is critically important with Lexis.com, Westlaw Classic, and other search engines that are very literal. If the author of a particular document did not use the exact term you are searching for, that document will not appear in your results.

Next, modify the search terms with expanders and placeholders so that a search will find variations of your words. The exclamation point expands words beyond a common root. For example, *employ!* will find employee, employer, employed, employs, employing, etc. The asterisk serves as a placeholder for an individual letter. Up to three asterisks can be used in a single term. This symbol is helpful when you are not sure which form of the word is used, or when you are not sure of the spelling of a word. For example, the search term *dr*nk* will find drink, drank, and drunk. Placeholders are preferable to the expander in some instances. Using an expander on *trad!* with hopes of finding *trade, trading, trades*, etc. will also produce results that include *traditional*. A better search term may be *trad****.

2. Add Connectors

Connectors determine where search terms will be placed in relation to one another in targeted documents. Effective use of connectors is critical in finding relevant authority. Even minimally

Table 2-4. Connectors and Commands

Goal	Lexis	Westlaw
Find alternative terms anywhere in the document	or	or blank space
Find both terms anywhere in the document	and &	and &
Find both terms within a particular distance from each other	/p = in 1 paragraph /s = in 1 sentence /n = within *n* words	/p = in 1 paragraph /s = in 1 sentence /n = within *n* words
Find terms used as a phrase	leave a blank space between each word of the phrase	put the phrase in quotation marks
Control the hierarchy of searching	parentheses	parentheses
Exclude terms	and not	but not %
Extend the end of a term	!	!
Hold the place of letters in a term	*	*

sophisticated combinations of parentheses and the various connectors can make your searches much more effective. Table 2-4 summarizes the most common connectors used on Lexis and Westlaw.

Most connectors are the same for the two services. However, two differences can cause some confusion. On Lexis.com, searching alternative terms requires the use of the connector "or." On Westlaw Classic, a blank space is interpreted as "or," although typing in that connector will produce the same result. The second difference concerns phrases or terms of art. Lexis.com reads a blank as joining words in a phrase. By contrast, to search a phrase on Westlaw Classic, the terms must be enclosed in quotation marks.

In both services, parentheses are used to refine terms-and-connectors searches. Note the following example: *(covenant or contract)*

/p (noncompetition or "restraint of trade") /p employ! This search will
look for paragraphs that contain either of the terms (covenant or contract), and either of the terms (noncompetition or "restraint of
trade"), and variations of the terms employ, employee, employer, employment, etc. Without the parentheses, the search may treat the example as a request for any one of the following three options: (1) the
word "covenant"; (2) "contract" within the same paragraph as "noncompetition"; or (3) the phrase "restraint of trade" within the same
paragraph as variations of employ, employee, etc.

3. Choose Sources or Databases

Terms-and-connectors searches are typically conducted in the full
text of documents to look for exact matches. Thus, to begin searching in a service with multiple databases, you must choose which
subset of that provider's resources to search. Your research will be
more efficient if you restrict each search to the smallest subset of
databases that will contain the documents needed. In addition,
searches in the smaller subsets are typically less expensive than
searches in vast databases.

Lexis.com and Westlaw Classic divide their resources into subsets
by type of document, topic, and jurisdiction. In Lexis.com, these
groups are simply called "sources." In Westlaw Classic, information is
grouped into "databases." Both services have directories to allow you
to browse among the sources and databases that are available for research. Clicking on the "i" next to the name of a source or database
will provide information about its scope. Note that the list of sources
or databases shown on a particular page may not include all that are
available. On Lexis.com, you may need to click on "View more
sources." On Westlaw Classic, you may need to add more databases
to those shown on a particular tab.

4. Restrict the Search with "Segments" and "Fields"

With terms-and-connectors searching, both Lexis.com and Westlaw Classic allow you to search specific parts of documents, such as
the date, author, or court. On Lexis.com, these specific parts are called

document *segments*; on Westlaw Classic, they are called *fields*. These options can be applied through drop-down menus. A segment or field term is added to the basic search with an appropriate connector. Two examples demonstrate the usefulness of segment and field searching. First, in conducting a full-text search, you can ensure that the results directly address your topic by searching the syllabi or synopses of the documents. Because this segment or field summarizes the contents of the document, your terms will appear there only if they are the focus of the document. Thus, the search will weed out documents where your terms are mentioned only in passing or in a footnote. Second, if you know the author of a relevant opinion or article, you can search for her name in the appropriate segment or field, eliminating documents where the person is referred to only tangentially.

5. Refine or Broaden the Search

With a query of terms and connectors, a search may result in a reasonable number of highly relevant documents, or no documents, or more than 1,000 documents. In the latter two instances, refining the search is necessary. When a search produces no results, use broader connectors (e.g., search for terms in the same paragraph rather than in the same sentence), use more general terms, or use a larger set of sources or a larger database. When a search produces a long list of results, skim them to see whether they are on point. If the results seem irrelevant, modify or edit the search query by using more specific terms, more restrictive connectors, or a smaller set of sources or databases.

The "Focus" feature on Lexis.com and the "Locate" feature on Westlaw Classic can be used to narrow results further. These features allow a researcher to construct a new search within a prior search, and produce a more refined subset of the initial search results. These features can be very cost efficient because they do not result in the additional charges of a new search. Indeed, a good strategy may be to create a broader initial search than you otherwise might and plan to conduct a series of restricting searches on the results.

6. Example Terms-and-Connectors Search

Continuing the example from Chapter 1, the following Westlaw Classic search uses the tools described above in a database containing California cases (abbreviated CA-CS): "negligent infliction of emotional distress" & da(aft 1990). The search will look for the phrase "negligent infliction of emotional distress" in documents published after 1990. After reviewing some of the documents returned in the search, you may decide to refine the search by using the "Locate" feature to restrict to documents containing the words spouse, husband, or wife. If the results are still not sufficiently focused on your topic, consider adding narrower terms.

E. Topic Searching Online

Sophisticated online search engines and services have tools for topic searching. The most user-friendly of these tools allow the researcher to begin with a list of broad areas of law and narrow the topic by clicking through successive lists.

Topic searching on Lexis.com uses the tool "Search by Topic," available from the "Search" screen, while Lexis Advance has a link "Browse Topics" at the top of every screen. On Westlaw Classic, this topic searching tool is called "KeySearch," which is accessed through the "Key Numbers" link at the top of any screen.

In the older services, Lexis.com and Westlaw Classic, you have the option of entering terms into a search box or clicking through lists of topics. To continue the workers' compensation example above, on Westlaw's KeySearch, you could enter the term "workers' compensation" in the search box. The search results would be the topics in KeySearch that contain that term. Alternatively, on either service you could click through successive layers of topics, moving from the general to the specific. Following this approach, you may select the broad topic "Employment Law," then narrow the topic to "Workers' Compensation," and finally choose "Injuries Covered." Under either approach, the final screen requires you to select a jurisdiction, such as California state cases, before running the search.

Using Lexis Advance, topic searching is slightly different. After clicking on "Browse Topics" at the top of the page, you can either select one of the topics listed or enter search terms in a box. If you select one of the topics (e.g., "Workers' Compensation"), you will be able to open its subtopics and eventually "Get topic documents" using a drop-down menu. If instead you enter search terms, the results will show how many hits appear in each of the topics listed on the initial page. You can open each topic and review the subtopics that contain your search terms. Again, clicking on the subtopics will allow you to select "Get topic documents." Under either approach, you can filter the resulting documents using the techniques discussed earlier.

F. Working with Online Documents

In most online services, you can move through the document either by scrolling through pages or by clicking through search terms. If the search term feature is not available, try using the "Find" feature on your web browser. Some services allow for book browsing, so that you can see the previous or next page of a set of documents. Reviewing nearby documents through book browsing can help provide context to the original document you were viewing.

One advantage to working in Lexis Advance and WestlawNext is the ability to highlight, annotate, and save documents in a system of folders. After creating folders and adding documents to them, you can access the folders and documents from any computer or mobile device. You can also share folders with co-workers.

G. Printing, Downloading, or Emailing Results

Both classic and current versions of Lexis and Westlaw allow you to download or email documents in addition to printing them. These options are effective early in a research project because they allow you to skim quickly to the point where your terms appear, using the

"Find" function. Given the ability to highlight and annotate text on either Lexis Advance or WestlawNext, or using your word processing program, you may choose to read and organize your research documents entirely on your computer.

However, many researchers still find it easier to read documents carefully on paper as opposed to the computer screen, and some prefer having key authorities in print on their desks rather than in separate documents on their computer's desktop. Even so, given the recent move of Westlaw to no longer support free printing in law schools, students should exercise caution in deciding which documents are truly needed in print.

H. Keeping Track

Many online services provide lists of past searches and results, and you should form the habit of printing or saving them. On Lexis.com, click "History." On Westlaw Classic, click "Research Trail." Lexis Advance and WestlawNext both provide "History" links that store your searches and results for periods ranging from three months to a year. On Lexis Advance, it is available from the "My Workspace" dropdown menu; on WestlawNext, the "History" link is available at the top right of every screen.

Chapter 11 of this book offers suggestions for keeping track of your research process and the documents that it produces. You might want to take a look at that chapter now, even though some of the details may not be clear until you've read the intervening chapters.

III. Other Online Research Services

Lexis and Westlaw are still the premier online tools for legal research because they provide the most documents and the most advanced search techniques. But other providers offer services that might suit your needs. Often these other online services provide more limited content than Lexis and Westlaw, but at more economical prices.

Four of these fee-based services are Fastcase, Casemaker, Loislaw, and VersusLaw. Their content is not as extensive as that of Lexis or Westlaw services, and their search mechanisms tend to be less user-friendly, but their prices are lower. VersusLaw, for example, offers an inexpensive monthly plan that includes federal and state materials and a basic citator service. Some bar associations make either Casemaker or Fastcase available for free to their members, although California does not.

One helpful online site with free material for anyone is Google Scholar. It provides access to state and federal cases, as well as law review articles. There is a rudimentary citator, but the site does not currently include statutes, administrative regulations, or other legal documents.

Bloomberg Law is gaining in popularity and market share among legal researchers, but currently its real edge is in transactional research. Searching Bloomberg feels like searching with Lexis Advance and WestlawNext because there is a single search bar (called the <GO> bar) and tabs for limiting the search (e.g., jurisdiction, content type, and practice area). However, the Bloomberg search looks for exact matches, while Lexis Advance and WestlawNext have more sophisticated algorithms. Bloomberg provides a citator called BCite.

Note that each online provider might have its own unique search techniques or commands. As one example, Westlaw Classic looks for terms within a paragraph when it sees the connector /p, while Bloomberg would perform that search only when it saw the connector p/. Reviewing a "help" or "tips" link is usually the best place to begin working with an unfamiliar service.

Chapter 3

Judicial Opinions[1]

Although case law is at the bottom of the hierarchy of primary authority, the ultimate goal of much legal research is to find cases that have interpreted and applied constitutions, statutes, and regulations. Thus, this book begins to explore primary authority with a discussion of judicial opinions — informally called cases — so you can better understand how to research the other sources of law discussed in succeeding chapters.

Courts write judicial opinions to explain their decisions in litigated disputes. Cases are published in rough chronological order in books called *reporters*. Some reporters include only cases decided by a certain court, for example, the California Supreme Court. Other reporters include cases from courts within a specific geographic region, for example, the western United States.[2] Reporters are fundamental tools of legal research, regardless of whether a researcher is using print or online sources, because cases are most often cited to print reporters, even by online services.

This chapter begins with an overview of the California and federal court systems. Then it explains reporters and the features added to opinions when they are published in reporters. The chapter ends with suggestions for reading cases effectively. The next chapter discusses how to use digests and online resources to find cases in conducting legal research.

---

1. Portions of this chapter are drawn from *Oregon Legal Research* by Suzanne E. Rowe and are used with permission.

2. Still other reporters publish only those cases that deal with a certain topic, such as bankruptcy, or the rules of civil and criminal procedure.

I. Court Systems

The basic court structure includes a trial court, an intermediate court of appeals, and an ultimate appellate court, often called the "supreme" court.[3] These courts exist at both the state and federal levels.[4]

A. California Courts

The trial courts of California are called *superior courts*. There is a superior court in each of the state's fifty-eight counties. Most counties have multiple court locations, so there are more than 450 trial court locations around the state. Most of the cases in the state system begin in a superior court. These courts hear cases concerning civil, criminal, family, probate, and juvenile matters.[5]

The state's intermediate courts are called *courts of appeal*. The state is divided into six districts. The headquarters of the six districts are provided in Table 3-1. The California Courts of Appeal have appellate jurisdiction over cases decided by the superior courts and by certain administrative agencies. They have original jurisdiction in a few areas, such as habeas corpus. Only a small percentage of the decisions by the courts of appeal are published.

---

3. The following discussion omits tribal courts in California. Information is available online for a number of tribal courts. Links are available from the National Indian Law Library, at http://narf.org/nill (click on "Tribal Law" then "Tribal Law Gateway"); the Tribal Court Clearinghouse, at www.tribalinstitute.org; California Indian Legal Services, at www.calindian.org; and the California Indian Law Association, at www.calindianlaw.org.

4. Not all states have the three-tier court system of California and the federal judiciary; some do not have an intermediate appellate court. Moreover, in some state systems the highest court is not called the "supreme" court. In New York, for example, the "Court of Appeals" is the highest court, and the trial court is called the "Supreme Court."

5. Prior to 1998, California trial courts were divided into superior and municipal courts. Following a constitutional amendment, trial courts were able to unify into superior courts that hear all types of cases. Each of the fifty-eight counties has now moved to the unified system.

Table 3-1. Districts of the California Courts of Appeal

District	Headquarters
First Appellate District*	San Francisco
Second Appellate District*	Los Angeles
Third Appellate District	Sacramento
Fourth Appellate District*	San Diego
Fifth Appellate District	Fresno
Sixth Appellate District	San Jose

* These three districts are subdivided into divisions.

California's highest court is the California Supreme Court. This court is located in San Francisco, although it regularly hears cases in Los Angeles and Sacramento, too. The California Supreme Court has seven justices. It has discretion to review cases decided by the courts of appeal, and it exercises that discretion to hear only cases involving significant questions of law or uniform application of the law. This court must, however, hear cases involving the death penalty. These cases are appealed directly from the superior courts to the California Supreme Court.

Cases decided by the California Supreme Court are mandatory authority in all lower courts in the state. Cases decided by any of the six courts of appeal are mandatory authority in all superior courts, whether or not the superior court is in the geographical district of a particular court of appeal. Because decisions of one court of appeal are not binding on the other five courts of appeal, it is possible to find conflicting decisions among the six districts. In those instances, superior courts may follow the decision of any court of appeal,[6] but as a practical matter most follow the decision of the court of appeal in whose district the superior court sits.[7] Eventually, the California

---

6. *Auto Equity Sales, Inc. v. Super. Ct. of Santa Clara Co.*, 57 Cal. 2d 450, 456 (1962).

7. *McCallum v. McCallum*, 190 Cal. App. 3d 308, 315 n. 4 (2d Dist. 1987).

Supreme Court is likely to settle the issue by granting review in a case addressing the issue.

The California courts' website at www.courts.ca.gov provides information about the courts, their jurisdiction, their locations, their calendars, and much more. The link "About California Courts" is a good place to begin.

B. Federal Courts

In the federal judicial system, the trial courts are called United States District Courts. There are ninety-four district courts in the federal system, with each district contained in a particular state. California is divided into four federal districts: northern, central, southern, and eastern. A state with a relatively small population may not be subdivided into smaller geographic regions. The entire state of Oregon, for example, makes up the federal District of Oregon.

The federal system's intermediate appellate courts are called United States Courts of Appeals. The country is divided into thirteen federal circuits.[8] California is in the Ninth Circuit, so cases from the United States District Courts located in California are appealed to the United States Court of Appeals for the Ninth Circuit. This circuit encompasses Alaska, Arizona, California, Hawaii, Idaho, Montana, Nevada, Oregon, and Washington, as well as Guam and the Northern Mariana Islands.

The highest court in the federal system is the United States Supreme Court. It decides cases concerning federal law (e.g., the United States Constitution and federal statutes). This court does not have the final say on matters of purely state law; that authority rests with the highest court of each state. Parties who wish to have the U.S. Supreme Court hear their case must file a petition for *certiorari*, as the court has discretion over which cases it hears.

As in the California court system, decisions of the highest court in the federal system are mandatory authority in all federal courts below

---

8. A map showing the federal circuits and linking to their websites is available at www.uscourts.gov/Court_Locator.aspx.

it (and on state courts hearing issues of federal law). Unlike the California system, however, decisions of the intermediate courts of appeals are mandatory authority in trial courts within only that circuit. For example, a decision of the Ninth Circuit Court of Appeals is mandatory authority on district courts in California but only persuasive authority in district courts in Virginia, which is in the Fourth Circuit.

The website for the federal judiciary is www.uscourts.gov.

II. Reporters

A. Reporters for California Cases

The California Constitution requires that all opinions issued by the California Supreme Court must be published. The official reporter (i.e., the reporter published by, or under contract with, the state) for these cases is *California Reports*. California Court of Appeal opinions are published in a separate official reporter called *California Appellate Reports*. Only some Court of Appeal cases are published. Opinions that are not published in *California Appellate Reports* are considered "unpublished" and may not be cited and generally should not be used in any manner.[9] Cases from state trial courts in California are not published and therefore cannot be cited or referred to; in fact,

---

9. Cal. R. Ct. 8.1115. There are two other instances when cases cannot be cited or quoted. The first instance is a Court of Appeal case that has been accepted for review by the Supreme Court or in which the Supreme Court has reached a decision. The second instance is when the Supreme Court orders a Court of Appeal case "depublished" because one of the parties has asked for depublication or the Supreme Court disagrees with the reasoning of the case. Depublished cases can often be found in *West's California Reporter* and *Pacific Reporter*, and on Westlaw or Lexis, but these cases will not appear in the bound official reporter. Because these cases were assigned pages in the advance sheets, the official reporter pages will be blank, with a notice that the case has been depublished. The depublication system is governed by Cal. R. Ct. 8.1125.

few states publish opinions at the trial court level. Unpublished opinions may be obtained directly from the court that decided the case.

As noted, *California Reports* and *California Appellate Reports* are the official reporters for California appellate cases. Cases from these courts are also reported in two commercially produced, unofficial reporters called *Pacific Reporter* and *West's California Reporter*, both published by West. In 1960, West stopped publishing California Court of Appeal cases in *Pacific Reporter* when it began publishing *West's California Reporter*. California Supreme Court cases are also still published in *Pacific Reporter*, as well as in *West's California Reporter*. While the text of the court's opinion is the same in the official and unofficial reporters, the appearance, pagination, and editorial additions are different. Table 3-2 lists the various reporters for California's appellate cases.

Table 3-2. Reporters for California Appellate Cases*

Court	Reporter Name	Abbreviation
California Supreme Court	*California Reports* (official)	Cal., Cal. 2d, Cal. 3d, Cal. 4th
	Pacific Reporter	P., P.2d, P.3d
	West's California Reporter	Cal. Rptr., Cal. Rptr. 2d, Cal. Rptr. 3d
California Courts of Appeal	*California Appellate Reports* (official)	Cal. App., Cal. App. 2d, Cal. App. 3d, Cal. App. 4th
	Pacific Reporter (through 1959)	P., P.2d, P.3d
	West's California Reporter (since 1960)	Cal. Rptr., Cal. Rptr. 2d, Cal. Rptr. 3d

* Some opinions of the Superior Court Appellate Division are published in a separate section of *California Appellate Reports*.

Commercial reporters often combine several courts' opinions under a single title. *Pacific Reporter* publishes cases from the courts of the following fifteen states: Alaska, Arizona, California, Colorado, Hawaii, Idaho, Kansas, Montana, Nevada, New Mexico, Oklahoma, Oregon, Utah, Washington, and Wyoming.[10] *Pacific Reporter* includes cases from the intermediate and highest appellate courts of most of these states. Other regional reporters are *North Eastern Reporter, Atlantic Reporter, South Eastern Reporter, Southern Reporter, South Western Reporter,* and *North Western Reporter.* All of these regional reporters are published by West. Because the publisher decided which states to group together in regional reporters, these groupings have no legal impact. Moreover, the coverage of each regional reporter is not the same as the composition of the federal circuits.

Reporters are published in *series.* Cases currently being published in *California Reports* and *California Appellate Reports* are appearing in the fourth series. *Pacific Reporter* and *West's California Reporter* are each in the third series. To find a case in a reporter with multiple series, whether searching in print or online, you must know which series the case was reported in. This information is included in the citation to the case, as explained below.

Cases are published electronically on a number of websites. The opinions of courts in California and the rest of the United States can be found on Westlaw and Lexis.[11] Court opinions can also be found on FindLaw, which is owned by West. Finally, the opinions of California courts are published on the official website of the courts,

---

10. If a state does not publish its own reporter, the regional reporter may be the official reporter. For example, the official reporter of Alaska cases is *Pacific Reporter.* The publisher, West, also publishes an offprint of *Pacific Reporter* that contains only Alaska cases. It is called *Alaska Reporter.* The appearance, pagination, and editorial aids are exactly like those in *Pacific Reporter,* but the volumes contain only those pages that report cases from Alaska courts.

11. In this book, general references to Lexis include both the Lexis.com service (which is being phased out) and Lexis Advance, while general references to Westlaw include both Westlaw Classic and WestlawNext. These services are available to law students through their school's subscription. While the students are not charged, the schools pay fees that are negotiated based on prior usage.

www.courts.ca.gov, under the "Opinions" link. This website is linked to a site maintained by LexisNexis, the publisher of the official reporters for California cases. Unlike the fee-based websites Lexis.com and Lexis Advance, this website is free. It includes a search function, but it does not include any of the editorial enhancements (explained in Features of a Reported Case, later in this chapter) that appear in the fee-based service. It is maintained primarily for citizens of California who are doing their own research, not for lawyers.

1. Citing California Cases

A citation to a California case requires the names of the parties, the volume and abbreviation for the reporter, the initial page of the case, and the year the case was decided.[12] *California Reports* is abbreviated as "Cal." The case *People v. Davis*, 18 Cal. 4th 712 (1998), can be found in volume 18 of the fourth series of *California Reports*, starting on page 712. The case was decided in 1998. The abbreviation for *California Appellate Reports* is "Cal. App." The case *People v. Wise*, 25 Cal. App. 4th 339 (1st Dist. 1994), was published in volume 25 of the fourth series of *California Appellate Reports*, beginning on page 339. It was decided in 1994 by the Court of Appeal for the First District.

In California, all documents submitted to a California court must cite to the official reporter; citation to additional reporters is optional.[13] For documents that are not going to be submitted to a California court, lawyers usually follow the custom of their firm or office. Especially when writing a memo for a firm outside of California, you would likely cite California cases to *Pacific Reporter* or *West's California Reporter*. To indicate which state's courts decided cases cited

---

12. The following citations adhere to the style of the *ALWD Manual*, which often is identical to the practitioner style used under the *Bluebook*. Beginning with the 5th edition of the *ALWD Manual*, all citations will be identical to the styles used in the *Bluebook*. For formats adhering to the *California Style Manual* or the *Bluebook*'s rules for law review articles, see Chapter 12.

13. Cal. R. Ct. 3.1113(c).

to a regional reporter, include an abbreviation at the beginning of the date parenthetical.

EXAMPLES: *People v. Davis*, 958 P.2d 1083 (Cal. 1998).

State v. Warner, 696 P.2d 1052 (Or. 1985).

Sometimes you will want to include citations to all reporters that have published an opinion. Multiple citations that refer to the same case in different reporters are called *parallel citations*.

EXAMPLES: *People v. Davis*, 18 Cal. 4th 712, 958 P.2d 1083, 76 Cal. Rptr. 2d 770 (1998).

State v. Warner, 298 Or. 640, 696 P.2d 1052 (1985).

Note that the California Supreme Court case has three parallel citations, whereas the Oregon case has only two parallel citations. Because California Courts of Appeal cases are no longer published in *Pacific Reporter*, a California Court of Appeal case will have only two parallel citations. Finally, note that the official reporter is always cited first among parallel citations.

2. Features of a Reported Case

The following discussion relates to cases published in *West's California Reporter* or *Pacific Reporter*. Both of these reporters are published by the same publisher; therefore, this discussion of the features of a reported case applies to all of the unofficially reported California cases and generally to all cases published in West reporters nationally. Knowing how West organizes its cases will also provide you with the tools to understand what you see in a case published by a different publisher or available online.

A case printed in a reporter contains the exact language of the court's opinion. Additionally, the publisher includes supplemental information intended to aid researchers in learning about the case, locating the relevant parts of the case, and finding similar cases. Some of these research aids are gleaned from the court record of the case, while others are written by the publisher's editorial staff. Most reporters will include most of these items, though perhaps in a different order. To best understand the following discussion, refer to a volume of *West's California Reporter*, preferably a volume containing a case you are familiar with. Alternatively, refer to the case excerpt in Figure 3-1 for examples of the concepts explained below. You could review the same case online using Westlaw Classic or WestlawNext; it will contain similar information, but the information will look different. To provide comparisons between online products from different publishers, two appendices to this chapter show the first screen of the case as it appears on WestlawNext and Lexis Advance.

Parallel citation. The reporter provides the citation for the case in any official or other unofficial reporter in which the case is also printed.

Parties and procedural designations. Most reported cases are from appellate courts. The appealing party is called the *appellant;* the other party is the *respondent.*[14]

Docket number. The docket number is a series of letters and numbers assigned by a court for keeping track of documents pertaining to a particular case. A case will have a different docket number in each court that hears the case.

Deciding court. The opinion gives the full name of the court that decided the case. For cases from the courts of appeal, this information includes both the district and, where appropriate, the division.

Date of decision. Each case begins with the date the case was argued and submitted to the court, and the date of the court's decision. For citation purposes, only the year the case was decided is important.

Synopsis. The synopsis is a short summary of the key facts, procedure, legal points, and disposition of the case. Reading a synopsis can quickly tell you whether a case is on point. You cannot rely exclusively

---

14. In most jurisdictions, the terms appellant-appellee are used when a party has a right to appeal, while the terms petitioner-respondent apply to parties when the court has discretion to hear the appeal. California uses the term respondent for the non-moving party in both instances.

Figure 3-1. Case Excerpt in West Reporter

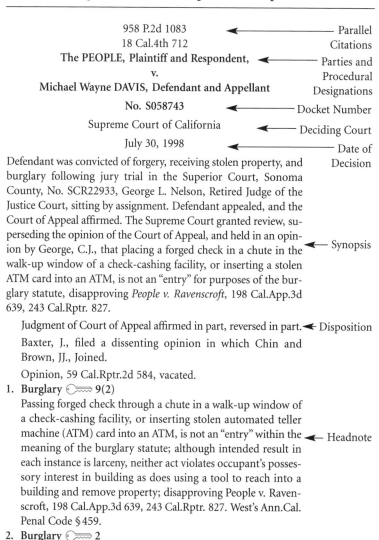

958 P.2d 1083 ←——————— Parallel
18 Cal.4th 712 Citations
The PEOPLE, Plaintiff and Respondent, ←——— Parties and
v. Procedural
Michael Wayne DAVIS, Defendant and Appellant Designations
No. S058743 ←——————— Docket Number
Supreme Court of California ←——— Deciding Court
July 30, 1998 ←——————— Date of
Decision

Defendant was convicted of forgery, receiving stolen property, and burglary following jury trial in the Superior Court, Sonoma County, No. SCR22933, George L. Nelson, Retired Judge of the Justice Court, sitting by assignment. Defendant appealed, and the Court of Appeal affirmed. The Supreme Court granted review, superseding the opinion of the Court of Appeal, and held in an opinion by George, C.J., that placing a forged check in a chute in the ←— Synopsis walk-up window of a check-cashing facility, or inserting a stolen ATM card into an ATM, is not an "entry" for purposes of the burglary statute, disapproving *People v. Ravenscroft*, 198 Cal.App.3d 639, 243 Cal.Rptr. 827.

Judgment of Court of Appeal affirmed in part, reversed in part. ←— Disposition Baxter, J., filed a dissenting opinion in which Chin and Brown, JJ., Joined.

Opinion, 59 Cal.Rptr.2d 584, vacated.

1. **Burglary** ⬡⇒ 9(2)
   Passing forged check through a chute in a walk-up window of a check-cashing facility, or inserting stolen automated teller machine (ATM) card into an ATM, is not an "entry" within the ←— Headnote meaning of the burglary statute; although intended result in each instance is larceny, neither act violates occupant's possessory interest in building as does using a tool to reach into a building and remove property; disapproving People v. Ravenscroft, 198 Cal.App.3d 639, 243 Cal.Rptr. 827. West's Ann.Cal. Penal Code § 459.

2. **Burglary** ⬡⇒ 2
   Burglary may be committed by using an instrument to enter a building, whether that instrument is used solely to effect entry, or to accomplish the intended larceny or felony as well. West's Ann.Cal.Penal Code § 459.

Source: *People v. Davis*, 76 Cal. Rptr. 2d 770 (Cal. 1985). Reprinted from *West's California Reporter* with permission of Thomson Reuters.

on a synopsis and you must never cite it, but it is a very useful research tool.

Disposition. The disposition of the case is the appellate court's decision to affirm, reverse, remand, or vacate the decision below. If the appellate court agrees with only part of the lower court's decision, the appellate court may affirm in part and reverse in part.

Headnotes. A headnote is a sentence or short paragraph that sets out a single point of law in a case. Most cases will have several headnotes. The text of each headnote often comes directly from the text of the opinion, but do not rely on headnotes in doing research and do not cite them in legal documents. Only the opinion itself is authoritative. At the beginning of each headnote is a number identifying it in sequence with other headnotes. Within the text of the opinion, the same sequence number will appear in bold print or in brackets at the point in the text supporting the headnote. Using these headnote numbers to find the point of law in the text is a quick way to locate particular points that interest you. You can think of each headnote's sequential number as a hyperlink in print.

Just after the sequence number, each headnote begins with a word or phrase, a key symbol, and a number. These are *topics* and *key numbers*, which are used in subject indexes to locate other cases that discuss similar points of law. These subject indexes, called *digests*, are discussed in Chapter 4.

Headnotes are generally the work of a given reporter's editorial staff, even when the text of the headnote is identical to language used in the opinion. Thus, the number of headnotes—and the text of the headnotes—will differ depending on which publisher's reporter you use. Because the official and unofficial reporters are published by different publishers, the headnotes in *California Reports* and *California Appellate Reports*, the official reporters, and the headnotes in *West's California Reporter* and *Pacific Reporter* are quite different.

Procedural information. West's California Reporter volumes contain a variety of procedural information. For example, those volumes indicate the court from which the case was appealed, the justices who heard the case, and the justice who wrote the decision. Note that following a justice's name will be "C.J." for the chief justice (or "P.J." for the presiding justice in the Court of Appeal) or "J." for another justice. If a case includes concurring or dissenting opinions, they will be noted in the procedural listings. This section also provides the names of the attorneys who argued for each party.

Opinion. In *West's California Reporter*, the actual opinion of the court begins immediately following the name of the justice who wrote the opinion. If the justices who heard the case do not agree on the outcome or the reasons for the outcome, there may be several opinions:

- *Majority opinion*: The opinion supported by a majority of the justices.

- *Concurring opinion*: An opinion that agrees with the outcome but not the reasoning of the majority.

- *Dissenting opinion*: An opinion written by a justice who disagrees with the outcome supported by the majority of the justices.

Other justices may join with the author of a concurring or dissenting opinion. While only the majority opinion is binding on future courts, the other opinions provide valuable insights and may be cited as persuasive authority. If there is no majority on both the outcome and the reasoning, the case will be decided by whichever opinion garners the most support, which is called a *plurality decision*. As a final alternative, a *per curiam* decision is written by the court; no single justice is given credit of authorship.

Cases decided by the California Supreme Court are heard by all seven of the sitting justices, unless a justice recuses himself or herself in a particular case. Cases decided by the California Courts of Appeal are heard by three justices sitting as a *panel* of the full court.[15] A party who does not agree with the decision of the panel may ask for a re-

---

15. Jurists on most intermediate appellate courts are called "Judges," but California uses the term "Justices."

hearing *en banc*, meaning that all of the justices on that court would rehear the case.

3. *Advance Sheets*

Publishers supply subscribers with softbound booklets called *advance sheets* that contain new cases, as well as some material that will not be published in bound reporters (e.g., the advance sheets for *West's California Reporter* report modifications to California Published Opinions; monthly updates to California civil and criminal jury instructions; and a summary of cases accepted for review by the Supreme Court). Once the bound volume containing those cases is published, the advance sheets are removed from the shelves. The pagination used in the advance sheets is the same as will be used in the hardbound volumes; thus, a citation to a case in the advance sheets will still be accurate after the case is published in hardbound volumes.[16]

4. *Other Sources for Finding California Cases*

A *slip opinion* is the actual document produced by the court, without the editorial enhancements normally added by the publisher. California Supreme Court cases are posted immediately upon filing. These opinions are normally filed at 10:00 a.m. on Mondays and Thursdays. California Court of Appeal opinions are routinely posted within a few hours of filing and may be filed any time during the day. Slip opinions are available either from the court that decided the case or online at www.courts.ca.gov/opinions.

---

16. As noted in footnote 9 and the accompanying text, depublished cases might appear in the advance sheets but might not appear in the bound version of the official reporter. In this situation, the reporter skips page numbers and notes that the case on the missing page numbers has been omitted. A similar notation accompanies cases when the Supreme Court has granted review. *West's California Reporter* often includes cases that have been ordered depublished; a footnote stating that the case was ordered depublished is sometimes included. Both Lexis and Westlaw indicate when a case has been depublished.

In addition, cases are added daily to both the Lexis and Westlaw services. Checking those websites is often the fastest way to find a new opinion, particularly one from a state other than California that may not post opinions as quickly.

B. Reporters for Federal Cases

Reporters are also published for cases decided by federal courts. Table 3-3 lists the federal court reporters, along with their citation abbreviations.

Table 3-3. Reporters for Federal Court Cases

Court	Reporter Name	Abbreviation
U.S. Supreme Court	*United States Reports* (official)	U.S.
	Supreme Court Reporter	S. Ct.
	United States Supreme Court Reports, Lawyers' Edition	L. Ed., L. Ed. 2d
U.S. Courts of Appeals	*Federal Reporter*	F., F.2d, F.3d
U.S. District Courts	*Federal Supplement*	F. Supp., F. Supp. 2d

Decisions of the United States Supreme Court are reported in *United States Reports* (official); *Supreme Court Reporter* (West); and *United States Supreme Court Reports, Lawyers' Edition* (LexisNexis). Although the official *United States Reports* should be cited if possible, that series frequently does not publish cases until several years after they are decided. Thus, for recent cases, lawyers often cite the *Supreme Court Reporter*. Another source for finding recent cases from the Supreme Court is *United States Law Week*. This service publishes the full text of cases from the Supreme Court and provides summaries of important decisions of state and federal courts.

Cases decided by the federal intermediate appellate courts are published in *Federal Reporter*, now in its third series. Some United States Courts of Appeals cases that were not selected for publication in *Federal Reporter*, and therefore might not be precedential, may be published in a relatively new reporter series, *Federal Appendix*. Selected cases from the United States District Courts, the federal trial courts, are reported in *Federal Supplement* and *Federal Supplement, Second Series.*

Supreme Court opinions are widely available online. The Court's website at www.supremecourt.gov includes slip opinions soon after the decisions are rendered, as well as opinions from 2007 to the present. Limited access to court of appeals and district court cases may be available from the individual court's website. An educational site supported by Cornell University also provides federal cases quickly; the address is www.law.cornell.edu/supct/. Lexis and Westlaw also publish federal opinions soon after they are released. Remember that Lexis and Westlaw make available "unpublished" opinions. Check court rules to determine the weight each court gives to unpublished opinions before citing one.

III. Reading and Analyzing Cases

Reading a case and analyzing its potential relevance to the problem you are researching can be challenging, time-consuming work. Lawyers spend hours reading (and re-reading) cases, especially in unfamiliar areas of law, when they may need to refer frequently to a law dictionary to try to understand the terms used. Using the following strategies should make reading and analyzing cases more effective.

A. Reading Cases Effectively

You should read a case at least three times: (1) to determine whether it is relevant; (2) to understand the case; and (3) to take notes on how it applies to your research problem.

First, review the synopsis quickly to determine whether the case seems relevant to your problem. If so, skim the headnotes to find the particular portion of the case that is relevant. Go directly to the portion of the case identified by the relevant headnote, skipping other portions initially, and decide whether it is important for your project.

If it is relevant, skim the entire case to understand what happened and why. You should still be focusing on the portion of the case identified by the relevant headnote, but you need the context of the entire case.

Second, after determining that a case is relevant, read the case slowly and carefully to understand its facts, analysis, and outcome. Skip the parts that are obviously not pertinent to your problem. At the end of each paragraph or page, consider what you have read. If you cannot summarize the concepts, try reading the material again.

Read the case a third time, this time taking notes. The notes may be as formal as a "case brief" or as informal as a list of points. Regardless of the form, the process of taking notes will help you parse through, identify, and comprehend the essential concepts of the case. If you have to write a legal document about your research problem, the notes will help you organize your analysis into an outline.

B. Analyzing the Substance of Cases

If a case involves legally significant facts that are similar to your client's situation and the court applies law on point for your problem, then the case is relevant and you should carefully consider the case as you analyze your problem. Legally significant facts are those that affect the court's decision. Some attorneys call these outcome-determinative facts or key facts. Which facts are legally significant depends on the case. The height of the defendant in a contract dispute is unlikely to be legally significant, but that fact may be critical in a criminal case where the only eyewitness testified that the thief was about five feet tall.

Even with the most thorough research, you are unlikely to find a case whose facts are identical to those of your client. Rather, you will find cases with more similar or less similar facts. Your job is to determine whether the case's facts are similar enough to your client's facts for the court to apply the law in the same way and reach the same result. If the outcome of the decided case favors your client's position, you will highlight the similarities. If the outcome of the decided case is not favorable from your client's perspective, you may argue that the case is distinguishable based on those factual differences, or you may argue that the reasoning of the decided case is faulty. Remember that you have an ethical duty to ensure that the court knows about a case directly on point from the controlling jurisdiction, even if the outcome of that case is adverse to your client.

It is also unlikely that one case will address all aspects of your client's situation. Most legal claims have several elements or factors. *Elements* are required subparts of a claim, while *factors* are important considerations, no one of which will decide the case. If a court decides that one element is not met, it might not discuss others. In a different case, the court may decide that two factors are so overwhelming that others have no impact on the outcome. In these circumstances, you would have to find other cases that analyze the remaining elements or factors.

After determining that a case is relevant to some portion of your analysis, you must decide how heavily that case will weigh in your analysis. You need to consider two important points here. One is the concept of *stare decisis*; the other is the difference between the *holding* of the case and *dicta* within that case.

Stare decisis means "to stand by things decided." This concept means that courts must follow prior opinions, ensuring consistency in the application of the law. *Stare decisis*, however, is limited to the courts within one jurisdiction. The Courts of Appeal of California must follow the decisions of the California Supreme Court but not those of the courts of any other state. The concept of *stare decisis* also applies to a court with respect to its own opinions. A court of appeal, thus, should follow its own earlier cases in deciding new matters. If a court decides not to continue following its earlier cases, it is usually because of changes in society that have outdated the law of the earlier case, or because a new statute has been enacted that changes the legal landscape.

Under *stare decisis*, courts are required to follow the *holding* of prior cases. The *holding* is the court's ultimate decision on the matter of law at issue in the case. Other statements or observations included in the opinion are not binding; they are referred to as *dicta*. For example, in deciding whether passing a bad check through the window at a bank's drive-through facility was burglary, a court observed that such a holding would mean a person putting his arm through a library chute to remove books would commit burglary. That observation was based on hypothetical facts and was not the basis of the court's decision. The observation is therefore dicta and is not binding on future courts, though it may be cited as persuasive authority.

After finding a number of relevant cases, you must synthesize them to state and explain the legal rule. Sometimes a court states the rule fully; if not, you must piece together the information from the relevant cases. Then use the analysis and facts of various cases to explain the law. Decide how the rule applies to the client's facts, and determine your conclusion. Note that this method of synthesis is much more than mere summaries of all the various cases.

Appendix 3-A. Case Excerpt on WestlawNext

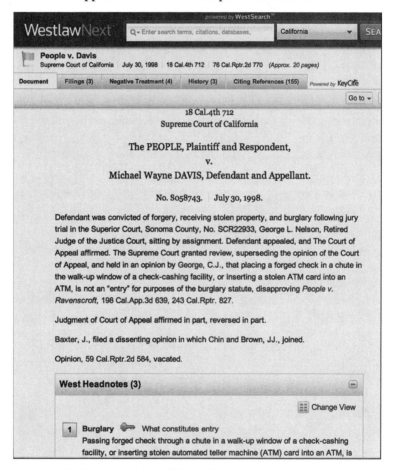

Source: Reprinted with permission of Thomson Reuters.

Appendix 3-B. Case Excerpt on Lexis Advance

▲ **People v. Davis, 18 Cal. 4th 712** (Copy citation)

Supreme Court of California
July 30, 1998, Decided
No. S058743.

Reporter: 18 Cal. 4th 712 | 958 P.2d 1083 | 76 Cal. Rptr. 2d 770 | 1998 Cal. LEXIS 4686 | 98 Cal. Daily Op. Service 5886 | 98 Daily Journal DAR 8209

THE PEOPLE, Plaintiff and Respondent, v. MICHAEL WAYNE DAVIS, Defendant and Appellant.

Prior History: Superior Court of Sonoma County. Super. Ct. No. SCR22933. George L. Nelson, Judge.
▣

Disposition: For the reasons discussed above, we conclude that defendant's placement of a forged check in the chute of the walk-up window of the check-cashing facility at issue cannot reasonably be termed an entry into the building for purposes of the burglary statute. Accordingly, the judgment of the Court of Appeal is reversed to the extent it affirms defendant's conviction for burglary, and affirmed in all other respects.

Core Terms

burglary, chute, forged check, air space, window, burglary statute, card, felony, check-cashing, burglarious entry, burglar, larceny, insertion, teller, stolen, walk-up, possessory right, accomplish, invitation, occupant's, forgery, door, felonious intent, burglary conviction, steal, business premises, remove property, outer boundary, perpetrator, effectuate

Case Summary

Procedural Posture
Defendant challenged the evidentiary sufficiency of the judgment of conviction for burglary, entered by the trial court and affirmed by the Court of Appeal (California), based upon evidence that defendant presented a stolen and forged check to the teller at a check-cashing business by placing the check in a chute in a walk-up window. Defendant had also been convicted of forgery and receiving stolen property.

Overview
Defendant was convicted of forgery, under Cal. Penal Code § 470, receiving stolen property under Cal. Penal Code § 469(c), and burglary, under Cal. Penal Code § 459, based upon evidence that he presented a stolen and forged check to the teller at a check-cashing business by placing the check in a chute in a walk-up window. Defendant maintained that the burglary conviction had to be reversed because he did not enter the check-cashing facility. The conviction was affirmed by the lower appellate court. The judgment was reversed. The court determined that the crucial issue was whether this was the type of entry the burglary statute was intended to prevent. The court looked to the interest sought to be protected by the burglary statute in general and the requirement of an entry in particular. Based on a review of the history of the offense of burglary, the court held that

Chapter 4

Researching Judicial Opinions

Because cases interpret constitutions, statutes, and administrative regulations, the most targeted way to find relevant case law is usually through annotations to resources that contain those primary sources, as explained in subsequent chapters. However, it is also possible to research case law directly, and it is necessary to do so when you research an issue based in common law. As with most legal research today, you can conduct your search using either print or electronic sources.

I. Digest Research

Print reporters organize cases chronologically, rather than topically. Therefore, publishers had to create a separate resource that organized cases by subject, similar to an index. The resource is called a *digest*; each digest contains multiple volumes that index cases by subject. Under each subject, the digest provides one or more headnotes from each case; each headnote points to a discussion of that subject in the case and provides a citation to the case. Because the digest is merely an index, it does not reprint the entire case. When using an online digest, the case is hyperlinked to the headnote.

This part of the chapter concentrates on digests published by West because they are the most widely used throughout the country. The discussion begins with print digests because they are the foundation of online products. Much of the information provided here would apply, however, to any other digests as well—both in print and online.

A. Print Digests

The digest most often used in California for researching California law is *West's California Digest 2d*. It includes headnotes of cases published in *West's California Reporter* from state courts in California, the same headnotes that appear at the beginning of the case itself in all West-published versions, including on Westlaw (see Figure 3-1 and Appendix 3-A, showing the headnotes in a case published by West). Headnotes from cases that originated in federal courts in California and were later decided by the Ninth Circuit and the United States Supreme Court are indexed here, too. This digest also includes references to opinions of the California attorney general and articles published by California law reviews. An example of entries in *West's California Digest 2d* is given in Figure 4-1.

Some digests index cases from a number of different jurisdictions. For instance, *Pacific Digest* contains headnotes of cases that are reported in *Pacific Reporter*, which were decided by many different state courts. Another digest, *Federal Practice Digest*, provides an index to cases decided by all federal trial and appellate courts. West's *Decennial Digest* indexes cases from all United States jurisdictions that are reported in West's national reporter system. Each of these digests is published by West and uses the West topic-key number system. Table 4-1 lists several digests useful in California research.

West's California Digest 2d includes headnotes for cases from 1950 to the present. Like many other digests, *West's California Digest 2d* is not cumulative, so you must look in the first edition, *West's California Digest*, for headnotes of cases decided between 1850 and 1950. Similarly, *Pacific Digest* publishes bound sets periodically; the most recent includes cases reported in volume 585 of *Pacific Reporter, Second Series* and subsequent volumes. To do thorough research in *West's California Digest*, *Pacific Digest*, and other non-cumulative digests, you may need to consult more than one series. Consider the period of time that is pertinent for your research, and then check the introductory information at the front of each digest to determine whether the digest covers that period. Notice also that digest volumes in the current series may include pocket parts, which provide a way for the

**Figure 4-1. Excerpts from *West's California Digest 2d*
"Adverse Possession"**

N.D.Cal. 1992. State satisfied elements of adverse possession for disputed park land under California law and, thus, logging company did not own land which it had purported to donate to state for charitable tax deduction, where state's occupation of property in dispute had continued for at least five years, and had been real, adverse to claims of others, and hostile to claims of others; state had marked boundary of park with signs, monuments, and other indicia of property being state park, and logging company had logged trees only up to indicated boundary of park. West's Ann.Cal.C.C.P. §§ 322, 325.

Kamilche Co. v. U.S., 809 F.Supp. 763, reversed 53 F.3d 1059, opinion amended on rehearing 75 F.3d 1391.

Cal. 1981. Elements necessary to establish title by adverse possession are tax payment and open and notorious use or possession that is continuous and uninterrupted, hostile to the true owner and under claim of title. West's Ann.C.C.P. § 325.

Gilardi v. Hallam, 636 P.2d 588, 178 Cal. Rptr. 624, 30 Cal.3d 317.

Cal.App. 3 Dist. 2011. The elements of adverse possession include: (1) possession must be by actual occupation under such circumstances as to constitute reasonable notice to the owner, (2) it must be hostile to the owner's title, (3) the holder must claim the property as his own, under either color of title or claim of right, (4) possession must be continuous and uninterrupted for five years, and (5) the holder must pay all the taxes levied and assessed upon the property during the period.

Hacienda Ranch Homes, Inc. v. Superior Court, 131 Cal.Rptr.3d 498, 198 Cal.App.4th 1122, as modified on denial of rehearing.

Cal.App. 4 Dist. 2011. To establish adverse possession, the claimant must prove: (1) possession under claim of right or color of title, (2) actual, open, and notorious occupation of the premises constituting reasonable notice to the true owner, (3) possession which is adverse and hostile to the true owner, (4) continuous possession for at least five years, and (5) payment of all taxes assessed against the property during the five-year period.

Main Street Plaza v. Cartwright & Main, LLC, 124 Cal.Rptr.3d 170, 194 Cal.App.4th 1044.

Table 4-1. Selected Digests

California Digest	Cases from California courts and federal courts in California (and appellate review of those cases)
Pacific Digest	Cases from states included in the *Pacific Reporter*
Decennial Digest	Cases from all jurisdictions included in West's national reporter system
Federal Practice Digest	Cases from United States District Courts, United States Courts of Appeals, and the United States Supreme Court (and some topical federal reporters)
United States Supreme Court Digest	Cases from the United States Supreme Court

publisher to include cases decided since the bound digest volume was published. When the publisher starts a new bound series, it creates the new series from the pocket parts, which can then be removed from the bound volumes. Your research in a digest is not complete until you have looked at the pocket parts to find the most recent cases.

B. Digest Features

The following discussion of the most important features of West digests also applies to cases on Westlaw. (See Appendix 4-A for an image of headnotes on WestlawNext.) Cases provided by LexisNexis on its electronic services have similar features, but the substance is different because the features are proprietary. (See Appendices 4-B and 4-C for images from Lexis Advance.) LexisNexis does not publish a system of print digests as West does. Nonetheless, familiarity with the West digest topic and key number and headnote features will make similar features familiar for LexisNexis's electronic resources.

1. Topics and Key Numbers

West digests index cases according to the West system of *topics* and *key numbers*. Westlaw uses the same system of topics and key numbers, which are uniform for all cases West publishes. West assigns a topic and key number to each headnote in a case, based on the legal point that is the focus of the headnote. The West *topic* places the headnote within a broad subject area of the law. Examples of West topics include "Criminal Law," "Health and Environment," and "Zoning and Planning." The *key number* relates to a subtopic within that area of law. For example, in the broad topic of "Criminal Law," key number 32 refers to the subtopic "Ignorance or mistake of law" as a defense. Cases on Westlaw have the same key number, but the topic of "Criminal Law" appears as the number 110.

"Criminal Law" is a vast topic, containing over 1,000 key numbers on subtopics covering criminal intent, defenses, pleas, trials, and sentencing guidelines. As an example of a much shorter topic, "Products Liability" includes approximately 100 key numbers on subtopics addressing products in general, particular products, and aspects of legal actions such as the burden of proof and the admissibility of evidence.

2. Headnotes

The bulk of each headnote entry is a sentence that summarizes the point of law that is the specific subject of the topic-key number assigned to that headnote. Each case is indexed in the digest under as many topics and key numbers as it has headnotes in the reporter.

In a digest, headnotes are arranged under each topic-key number according to the court that decided the case. Federal cases are listed first, followed by state cases. Within the federal and state systems, cases are listed according to judicial hierarchy: cases from the highest appellate court are listed first, followed by cases of intermediate appellate courts, then trial court cases. In *West's California Digest 2d*, cases from the California Courts of Appeal are organized starting with the first district and continuing through the sixth district in ascending numerical order. Cases from each court are given in reverse chronological order. This order is helpful because recent cases, which are listed first, are more likely to be pertinent to your research.

At the beginning of each headnote in the digest is a court abbreviation and date. The abbreviations are explained in tables at the beginning of each digest volume. At the end of the digest headnote are citations to any statutes that are cited in the case. This information is followed by the case citation and any parallel citations.

Although West may have assigned a topic-key number to a particular point of law, a given jurisdiction may not have decided a case on that point. In that instance, no entries will appear under the topic-key number of that jurisdiction's digest. However, the topic-key number system makes it easy to research cases in other jurisdictions using West digests and Westlaw, which may lead to persuasive authorities.

C. Using the Descriptive-Word Index

Once you have search terms, you are ready to look for cases by using the terms in the Descriptive-Word Index, which is contained in several volumes shelved at the end of the digest. (See Figure 4-2.) Record both the topic and the key number; many topics have the same key numbers, so a number alone is not a helpful research tool. Check each volume's pocket part for the most recent information. Note that some topics are abbreviated in the Descriptive-Word Index. A list of topics and their abbreviations is included at the front of each index volume.

Using the topics and key numbers you recorded from the Descriptive-Word Index, select a digest volume that contains one of the topics. At the beginning of each topic is a list of "Subjects Included" as well as "Subjects Excluded and Covered by Other Topics." These lists will help you decide whether that topic is likely to index cases most relevant to your research. After these lists is the key number outline of the topic, under the heading "Analysis," as seen in

Figure 4-2. Excerpts from the Descriptive-Word Index
in *West's California Digest 2d*

---

45 Cal D 2d-85   ADVERSE

References are to Digest Topic and Key Numbers

ADVERSE POSSESSION-Cont'd
HOSTILE possession, **Adv Poss**
  58-85, 114(1), 115(5), 116(5)
HUSBAND and wife,
  Married women, **Hus & W 69.5**
INDIAN lands, **Indians 22**
INSTRUCTIONS to jury,
  Adv Poss 116
INTERRUPTION of possession, **Adv**
  Poss 46-49
JOINT tenancy, **Joint Ten 9**
JUDGMENT,
  Color of title, **Adv Poss 74**
  Title or right to property,
    Adv Poss 51
JUDICIAL sales,
  Color of title, **Adv Poss 74**
JURY questions, **Adv Poss 115**
  Tenancy in common, **Ten in C 15(11)**

KNOWLEDGE or notice,
  Former owner, **Adv Poss 31**
LANDLORD and tenant, **Land &**
  Ten 66
LAWFUL possession element,
  Adv Poss 26
LEGATEES,
  Hostile character of possession,
    Adv Poss 62(1)
LICENSES,
  Possession after amicable entry,
    Adv Poss 60(2)
LIFE estates. See heading **LIFE ESTATES**
LIMITATIONS,
  Bar,
    Action for recovery of land,
      Adv Poss 106(2)
    Suspension of statute, **Adv Poss 45**

Source: *West's California Digest 2d.* Reprinted with permission of Thomson Reuters.

Figure 4-3. Many topics follow a general litigation organization, so that elements, defenses, pleadings, and evidence are discussed in that order. Take a moment to skim the Analysis outline, both to get an overview of the law and to ensure that you found in the Descriptive-Word Index all the relevant key numbers within that topic.

Next turn to each of the relevant key numbers and carefully review each of the case headnotes listed there. Write down the citation for each case that you decide you need to read. At this point, the cites do not have to be complete or conform to any system of citation.

**Figure 4-3. Excerpts from *West's California Digest 2d*
Analysis for "Adverse Possession"**

Analysis

I. NATURE AND REQUISITES, ☞1–95.
   (A) ACQUISITION OF RIGHTS BY PRESCRIPTION IN GENERAL,
      ☞1–13.
   (B) ACTUAL POSSESSION, ☞14–27.
   (C) VISIBLE AND NOTORIOUS POSSESSION, ☞28–33.
   (D) DISTINCT AND EXCLUSIVE POSSESSION, ☞34–38.
   (E) DURATION AND CONTINUITY OF POSSESSION, ☞39–57.
   (F) HOSTILE CHARACTER OF POSSESSION, ☞58–85.
   (G) PAYMENT OF TAXES, ☞86–95.
II. OPERATION AND EFFECT, ☞96–109.
   (A) EXTENT OF POSSESSION, ☞96–103.
   (B) TITLE OR RIGHT ACQUIRED, ☞104–109.
III. PLEADING, ☞110, 111.
IV. EVIDENCE, ☞112–114.
V. TRIAL, ☞115–117.

Source: *West's California Digest 2d*. Reprinted with permission of Thomson Reuters.

Recording the last name of one party, the volume, reporter, and page number will often be sufficient. Update your research with pocket parts and with softbound supplements shelved at the end of the digest. For same-day currency, you must go to an online service, such as those provided by Westlaw and Lexis.

Reviewing headnotes and recording possibly relevant case citations is time-consuming but critical work. To analyze a client's situation accurately, you need to read every relevant case; the cost of skipping a key case is high. However, you may be selective in deciding which cases to read first. Additionally, when a topic-key number contains many pages of case headnotes, or when you are working under tight deadlines, you may need to be selective in choosing the cases you are able to read. First, read those cases that are binding authority in your jurisdiction. Within that subset, read the most recent cases. If a headnote includes facts similar to your client's, read that case, too.

D. Starting with a Relevant Case

If you begin a research project knowing one case on point, read the case in a West reporter, and identify the headnotes that are relevant to your issue. In the print reporter, note the topic and key number given for each relevant headnote. Select a digest volume containing one of the relevant topics; within that topic, find the key number given in the related headnote. Under the key number, the digest will list all the headnotes of cases with that topic-key number. Repeat this step for each relevant topic-key number in your original case. Remember to update the search to find the most recent cases on point, using pocket parts and paper supplements.

You can also use a relevant case on Westlaw and Lexis to find more cases that are also relevant. While reading a case on WestlawNext, you will see that each headnote's topic and key number are hyperlinked to an online digest. Similarly, on Westlaw Classic, simply click on the topic and key number of the relevant headnote to search for additional cases that include the same area of law. Using Lexis Advance, the descriptive phrases preceding the headnotes link to documents on the same topic (from the drop-down menu, select "Get topic documents"). To find further cases on Lexis.com, click on the "All" icon at the end of the topic string in the "Lexis Headnotes" box near the beginning of the case. Finally, you can also use a citator, discussed in Chapter 9, to find additional cases that address the same point of law.

II. Online Research

A majority of case law research is done today online using a fee-based electronic service, a free electronic service provided by a government, or other websites. As clients become more and more cost-conscious, it pays to become familiar with multiple services, especially free online services.

This section first discusses Westlaw and WestlawNext, then Lexis.com and Lexis Advance, and then ends with a discussion of some free services accessible through the Internet. The general descriptions below will get you to the first results page of your search.

A. Westlaw Classic and WestlawNext

To begin a case law search on Westlaw Classic, you can click on "Directory" at the top of the page to get to the overall organization of materials on Westlaw. Materials are organized by type of material and by jurisdiction or geographical area. To find California cases, click on "Cases" under "U.S. State Materials," then open the folder for "Individual State and Other U.S. Jurisdictions." Choose one of the hyperlinks for California cases, which will lead to a search box in which you can enter either a terms-and-connectors search or a natural-language search, depending on which you choose.

You can do a search by key number on Westlaw Classic by clicking on "Key Numbers" at the top of the opening screen and then picking a jurisdiction in the next screen. You can use that screen to open the West Key Number Digest Outline or click on "KeySearch" to get to the list of key numbers by topic.

A search on WestlawNext begins with a search box at the top of the page. You can enter search terms to find cases in your area of interest or a case citation to get a particular case. Select a jurisdiction, for example California, in the box to the right of the search box and click on "Search." You can refine your search by clicking on one of the tabs below the "Browse" heading, which will allow you to choose federal or state materials, a particular area of law by clicking on "Topics," or access the West key number system by clicking on "Tools."

B. Lexis.com and Lexis Advance

Using Lexis.com, the opening page provides a lists of resources organized by type (e.g., cases, court records), by jurisdiction (e.g., federal or individual states), by area of law (e.g., bankruptcy, environment), and by secondary sources. To find California cases, click on "California" under the heading "State Legal—U.S." Under "Find Cases" on the next screen, you can choose among files organized by the court that decided the cases or click on "By Area of Law" at the bottom of the cases list. Either approach will take you to a search box in which you can enter either a terms-and-connectors search or a natural-language search.

Lexis Advance operates by having a single search box on its opening page. In addition to entering search terms in this box, you can limit your results using the tabs below it to choose a kind of source, a jurisdiction, and a practice area. To search just for cases, click on the left tab and select "Cases" under the heading for primary authority. To search for California cases, click on the center tab under the search box and select "California" as the jurisdiction in which you want to search. Using the right tab, you can also limit your search to a particular practice area or topic (e.g., family law or torts). Once you have chosen the limits you want to apply to your search, simply click on the "Search" button at the top of the page to begin looking for cases.

C. Other Online Sources of Case Law

The availability of case law on the Internet without having to pay a fee has increased rapidly in recent years, and the trend is likely to continue. More and more courts are posting both current and past cases on their websites. Sometimes, these sites do not allow searching by topic or search term, so you can look only for specific cases whose titles or docket numbers you already know.

The website for the California courts, www.courts.ca.gov, includes a fully searchable database through Lexis that is provided for the use of non-lawyers, although law students and lawyers can use it. The site allows you to search by natural-language search terms, by citation, by party name, and by judge. An advanced search feature allows you to use a terms-and-connectors search. The site provides the official reporter version of the cases but does not include any of the editorial enhancements found on Lexis products, such as headnotes and case summaries. You can pay to get those features by using a credit card.

Another free service is Google Scholar, found at scholar.google.com. On the home page, click on "Legal documents" below the search box and then choose between cases from federal courts or California courts; click on the link for "Select courts" to select courts from other jurisdictions. At that point, simply enter your search terms in the search box. Cases that come up in a Google Scholar search contain the full text of the case but do not include any of the editorial enhancements provided by Lexis or Westlaw. Running the same search without picking a court will bring up not only cases, but also secondary documents that relate to the search.

Appendix 4-A. Headnotes on WestlawNext

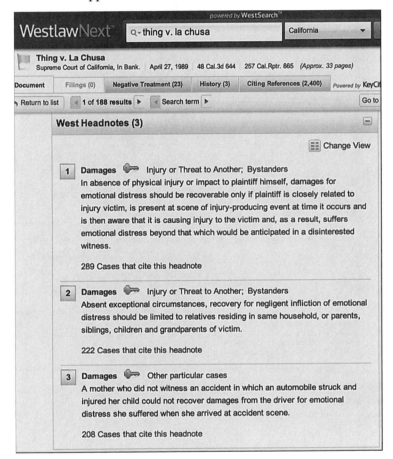

Source: Reprinted with permission of Thomson Reuters.

Appendix 4-B. Headnotes on Lexis Advance

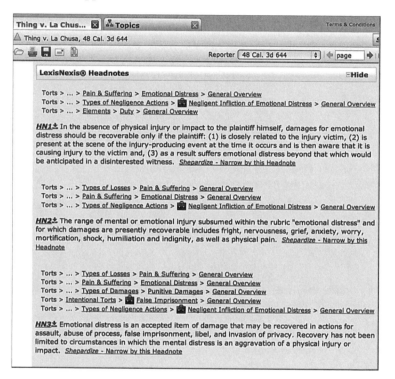

Source: Copyright LexisNexis 2013, a division of Reed Elsevier, Inc. All rights reserved. Lexis is a registered trademark of Reed Elsevier, Inc. and is used with permission of LexisNexis.

Appendix 4-C. Topic Link from Lexis Advance Headnotes

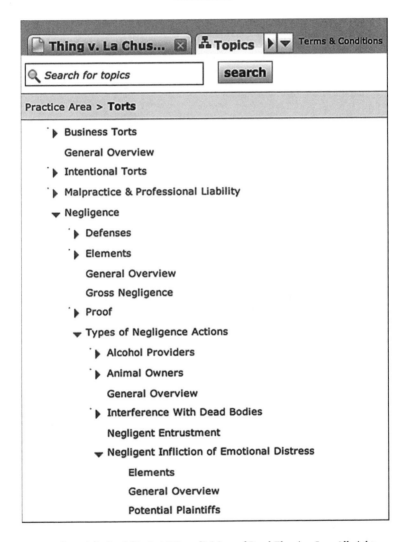

Chapter 5

Constitutions

California has had two constitutions. The first constitution was framed at a constitutional convention in September and October 1849 and ratified at an election on November 13, 1849, nearly a year before California became a state. A second constitutional convention met in 1879, and the voters ratified the new constitution on May 7, 1879. It became effective January 1, 1880, but is always referred to as the Constitution of 1879.

The provisions of the current California Constitution parallel many of the provisions of the United States Constitution, although the California Constitution provides for greater rights in some areas. Article I, section 1 lists the inalienable rights of California's citizens. Among those rights are "enjoying and defending life and liberty, acquiring, possessing, and protecting property, and pursuing and obtaining safety, happiness, and privacy."[1]

California has one of the longest constitutions in the United States because it covers many issues often thought of as being statutory in nature. (See Table 5-1.) For example, Article I, section 2 provides the news media with a shield against an adjudication of contempt by a judicial, legislative, or administrative body for refusing to disclose unpublished information or sources. Because of the breadth of issues covered by the California Constitution, it is always wise to consider whether a constitutional provision affects a particular research problem.

---

1. Cal. Const. art. I, §1.

Table 5-1. Articles of the Constitution of California

Article I	Declaration of Rights
Article II	Voting, Initiative and Referendum, and Recall
Article III	State of California
Article IV	Legislative
Article V	Executive
Article VI	Judicial
Article VII	Public Officers and Employees
Article IX	Education
Article X	Water
Article XA	Water Resources Development
Article XB	Marine Resources Protection Act of 1990
Article XI	Local Government
Article XII	Public Utilities
Article XIII	Taxation
Article XIIIA	[Tax Limitation]
Article XIIIB	Government Spending Limitation
Article XIIIC	[Voter Approval for Local Tax Levies]
Article XIIID	[Assessment and Property Related Fee Reform]
Article XIV	Labor Relations
Article XV	Usury
Article XVI	Public Finance
Article XVIII	Amending and Revising the Constitution
Article XIX	Motor Vehicle Revenues
Article XIXA	Loans from the Public Transportation Account or Local Transportation Funds
Article XIXB	Motor Vehicle Fuel Sales Tax Revenues and Transportation Improvement Funding
Article XX	Miscellaneous Subjects
Article XXI	Reapportionment of Senate, Assembly, Congressional and Board of Equalization Districts
Article XXII	[Architectural and Engineering Services]
Article XXXIV	Public Housing Project Law
Article XXXV	Medical Research

Note: Repealed and rejected articles are not listed.

I. Researching the California Constitution

You can research the California Constitution online using either Westlaw or Lexis or in either of the published statutory codes of California, *West's Annotated California Codes* and *Deering's California Codes Annotated*. In the print resources, the constitution appears in the first several volumes of both annotated codes. The index to the constitution appears in both code versions in the volume that contains the last section of the constitution. In electronic and print resources, the publishers have included additional documents, including the text of the Constitution of 1849, the U.S. Constitution, and various federal statutes affecting California, including the act for the admission of the state to the union. The two publishers have not included exactly the same additional documents, so if possible check materials from both publishers when looking for a specific document.

As explained in Chapters 1 and 2, begin your research by generating a list of research terms from the facts and issues of your problem. Use those terms in either a keyword search or in an index and then record the references given. For example, using the term "Searches and Seizures" leads to references to Article I, sections 13 and 24 of the California Constitution.

To find cases and other authorities that have discussed a certain provision of the state constitution, look for the editorial material that follows the text of the particular section of each relevant article. This material includes historical notes, cross-references to statutes, citations to relevant law review articles, references to other materials published by the same publisher, references to analogous sections of the U.S. Constitution, and case annotations. These case annotations are called "Notes of Decisions," and they reference cases and attorney general opinions. Each annotation contains a brief summary of the source referenced and its citation, which will enable you to locate the actual source. (See Figure 5-1.) Be sure not to rely on the short summary; reading the text of the source itself is the only way to analyze its relevance to your research.

Figure 5-1. Excerpt of Annotations for California Constitution

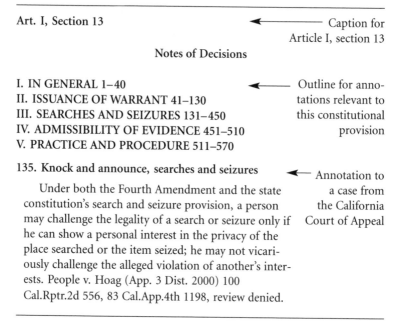

Art. I, Section 13   ◄————— Caption for
                                        Article I, section 13
                   Notes of Decisions

I. IN GENERAL 1–40   ◄——— Outline for anno-
II. ISSUANCE OF WARRANT 41–130   tations relevant to
III. SEARCHES AND SEIZURES 131–450   this constitutional
IV. ADMISSIBILITY OF EVIDENCE 451–510   provision
V. PRACTICE AND PROCEDURE 511–570

135. Knock and announce, searches and seizures   ◄— Annotation to
     Under both the Fourth Amendment and the state   a case from
constitution's search and seizure provision, a person   the California
may challenge the legality of a search or seizure only if   Court of Appeal
he can show a personal interest in the privacy of the
place searched or the item seized; he may not vicari-
ously challenge the alleged violation of another's interests. People v. Hoag (App. 3 Dist. 2000) 100
Cal.Rptr.2d 556, 83 Cal.App.4th 1198, review denied.

Source: *West's Annotated California Codes*, volume 1A, page 174 (2002). Reprinted with permission of Thomson Reuters.

The Notes of Decisions are divided into subject-matter categories chosen by the publisher. In Lexis, Westlaw, and *West's Annotated California Codes,* these categories are outlined at the beginning of the Notes of Decisions; there is no similar outline in *Deering's California Codes Annotated.* If the version you are using has an outline, begin research in the annotations by looking over the outline for the area that is most pertinent to your research. This initial scanning of the outline is particularly important for researching sections of the constitution that have been discussed in many cases and attorney general opinions, such as in the example in Figure 5-1. Note that the annotations listed in these sources do not represent every authority that may be relevant to your research. To find additional cases on point, use the strategies discussed in Chapter 4. Chapter 10 explains using secondary sources as research tools.

Finally, the California Constitution is also available online without charge on two state websites: www.leginfo.ca.gov/const.html and http://leginfo.legislature.ca.gov/faces/codes.xhtml (click on "California Constitutions" at the top of the list).[2] The websites contain links to a table of contents and a search engine that allows searching by keyword. Neither includes any case annotations or other editorial enhancements.

II. Interpreting the California Constitution

California courts interpret a constitutional provision by considering the intent of those who enacted it. "To determine that intent, courts look first to the language of the constitutional text, giving the words their ordinary meaning."[3] In determining the "ordinary meaning" of the words, California courts may look to dictionaries, including legal dictionaries, and to decisions of other courts considering the same or similar language.[4] However, the words of the constitutional provision "'must receive a liberal, practical common sense construction.'"[5] Moreover, the "literal language of enactments may be disregarded to avoid absurd results and to fulfill the apparent intent of the framers."[6]

When the language of the provision is not clear, California courts look to the source of the constitutional provision in interpreting its meaning. For provisions of the Constitution of 1879 that are still in effect, the court can look to the proceedings of the constitutional convention of 1879, as well as to the daily journal of the debates. Both are difficult to find in most libraries, although microfiche copies are available through the Congressional Information Services (CIS) *State Constitutional Conventions* set, which some libraries have.

---

2. The text of the Constitution of 1849 is available on the website for the State Archives at www.sos.ca.gov/archives/collections/1849/full-text.htm.

3. *Leone v. Med. Bd. of Cal.*, 22 Cal. 4th 660, 665 (2000).

4. *Id.* at 666.

5. *L.A. Metro. Transit Auth. v. Pub. Util. Comm'n*, 59 Cal. 2d 863, 869 (1963) (quoting *Co. of Alameda v. Sweeney*, 151 Cal. App. 3d 505, 512–13 (1st Dist. 1957)).

6. *Amador Valley Jt. Union High Sch. Dist. v. St. Bd. of Equalization*, 22 Cal. 3d 208, 245 (1978).

Because the current California Constitution has been amended repeatedly, your research is likely to involve a section that was not part of the Constitution of 1879. The constitution may be *revised* through a constitutional convention called by the legislature.[7] It may be *amended* through either a proposal passed by a two-thirds vote of each house of the legislature[8] or by a voter initiative;[9] in either case, voters then have the opportunity to approve or reject the proposal or initiative.[10] The distinction between revision and amendment relates to the scope of the proposed change, and it can be crucial to the viability of the attempted change. The California Supreme Court has held that revision, which is a more sweeping change to the constitution than amendment, must be done through a constitutional convention and may not be accomplished through the initiative process.[11]

In deciding a 2009 challenge to Proposition 8, the ballot initiative that amended the constitution to forbid recognition of same-sex marriages in the state, the court clarified the distinction between a revision and an amendment to the constitution.[12] The court identified a revision as one that works a "fundamental change in the *basic governmental plan or framework* established by the preexisting provisions of the California Constitution."[13] To be fundamental, a change must affect the structure of the state government "'or the foundational powers of its branches.'"[14] The court has only once found such a fundamental change in a voter-approved initiative in recent decades.[15] In that case, the initiative purported to order the court itself not to find greater protections for criminal defendants under the California Constitution than they could receive under the U.S. Constitution.[16] The

---

7. Cal. Const. art. XVIII, § 2. California has not had a constitutional convention since 1879.

8. Cal. Const. art. XVIII, § 1.

9. Cal. Const. art. XVIII, § 3.

10. Cal. Const. art. XVIII, § 4.

11. *McFadden v. Jordan*, 32 Cal. 2d 330, 332–33 (1948).

12. *Strauss v. Horton*, 46 Cal. 4th 364 (2009).

13. *Id.* at 441 (emphasis in original).

14. *Id.* (quoting *Legislature v. Eu*, 54 Cal. 3d 492, 509 (1991)).

15. *Raven v. Deukmejian*, 52 Cal. 3d 336, 356 (1990).

16. *Id.* at 350.

court deemed this limitation on its own powers to be a revision of the state's constitution.

The initiative process was adopted in a number of states during the Progressive Era in the early 20th century in response to legislative corruption. California adopted it in 1911, largely to address the control of the legislature by the railroad companies. This process allows voters to propose amendments to the state constitution by placing measures on the election ballot. Voters begin the process by submitting a petition with at least a certain number of signatures of qualified voters; this number is equal to 8% of the number of voters in the previous gubernatorial election (it is 5% for an initiative that proposes a statute).[17]

Because the initiative process has become increasingly popular since the success of the property tax initiative Proposition 13 in 1976, the ballot may contain more than one initiative that addresses the same subject. If the voters pass two or more conflicting initiatives in the same election, the constitution includes the unusual rule that the measure that received the highest number of votes in the election prevails.[18]

If a court must look behind the wording of a section of the constitution added or amended by voter initiative, it looks for evidence of the voters' intent in the ballot summary and the arguments and analysis presented in the California *Voter Information Guide*. That pamphlet is prepared before each election and distributed to all registered voters by the secretary of state. Complete sets of these pamphlets from 1911 forward may be found in a few larger libraries, but most law libraries are likely to have voter pamphlets from only the last decade or two. The California Secretary of State's Office maintains an electronic database of voter pamphlets dating back to March 1996 at www.sos.ca.gov; under "Elections," click on "Ballot Measures"

---

17. Cal. Const. art. II, §8(b). The lower percentage for statutes was approved by the voters in 1966 as an effort to encourage statutes rather than constitutional amendments. Joseph R. Grodin, Calvin R. Massey & Richard B. Cunningham, *The California State Constitution: A Reference Guide* 69–70 (1993).

18. Cal. Const. art. II, §10.

and then "Voter Information Guides." From that site, you can access a searchable database of California ballot measures dating back to 1911, maintained by the University of California Hastings College of Law, by clicking on a link at the bottom of the page. The Hastings site contains a word search to find specific voter pamphlets.

III. Locating the United States Constitution

The federal constitution is the foundational law of the United States. As noted above, it is published along with the California Constitution in both *Deering's California Codes Annotated* and *West's Annotated California Codes*. It is also available in print in the first several volumes of *United States Code Annotated* and *United States Code Service*. These series are explained in Chapter 6.

The U.S. Constitution is also available online at both state and federal websites. You can find the text of the Constitution or commentary on developments in constitutional law at the sites listed below.

- www.loc.gov/law/guide, a site maintained by the Law Library of Congress with links to a wide range of sites that include the text of the U.S. Constitution, as well as commentaries and annotations, some of which also provide search engines;

- www.findlaw.com/casecode/constitution, a free research site with a search engine; and

- www.scotusblog.com, a law blog written by lawyers, law professors, and law students that covers cases before the U.S. Supreme Court from certiorari through decision and live blogs during some oral arguments and when the Court announces opinions. The blog is supported by Bloomberg Law.

Chapter 6

Statutes

In the hierarchy of legal authority in the United States, statutes come just below constitutions and ahead of regulations and cases as controlling sources of law. Therefore, for almost any research problem, you should first check to see if there is a statute that affects your client's rights or responsibilities. Statutes create new rights or responsibilities when the legislature decides that the law needs to address a new issue, such as anti-discrimination laws or seat belt laws. The legislature has also taken many common law rights and duties and enacted them into statutory law. For example, criminal law has been made almost completely statutory, sometimes by enacting the common law elements, sometimes by changing the elements, and sometimes by creating new crimes, such as stalking.[1] Even if your client's problem is not governed by a statute, you may still need to consult the relevant code to find the statute of limitations that governs how long you have to bring a claim.

I. Researching California Statutes in Print

Despite the availability of online sources for California statutes, many attorneys find that statutory research is initially more effective using print codes. Moreover, some online sources are based on their print counterparts, so understanding research in print is helpful. This chapter begins with print sources then covers online sources for statutory research.

---

1. Section 646.9 of the California Penal Code defines and criminalizes stalking. It was added to the Penal Code in 1990.

Table 6-1. Outline for Statutory Research in Print

1. Look up research terms in the index of the appropriate statutory compilation to find references to relevant statutes.
2. Locate, read, and analyze the statutes in the main volumes. If there is a pocket part or paper supplement, check for recent changes in the language of the statute.
3. Refer to annotations following the statutory language to find citations to cases and other authorities that interpret, apply, or analyze the statute.
4. If the resource you are using has a pocket part or supplementary volume, check that for more recent annotations.
5. Read and analyze the relevant cases.

A. California Codes

California has two print statutory compilations: *Deering's California Codes Annotated*, published by LexisNexis, and *West's Annotated California Codes*, published by West. The language of the statutes should be identical in both sets, so you can use either version for your research. The research steps are the same in both versions, as outlined in Table 6-1.

California statutes can be enacted by either the legislature or the voters through the referendum and initiative process, which is similar to the initiative process for constitutional amendments, discussed in Chapter 5. Enacted statutes are then *codified*, meaning that they are grouped according to subject matter.[2] As each new statute is enacted, it is placed within the appropriate subject-matter code.

California statutes are grouped into twenty-nine individual subject-matter codes, which are listed in Table 6-2. Each of these

---

2. A few statutes and some initiative acts are never codified.

Table 6-2. California Statutory Codes

Business and Professions	Insurance
Civil	Labor
Civil Procedure	Military and Veterans
Commercial	Penal
Corporations	Probate
Education	Public Contract
Elections	Public Resources
Evidence	Public Utilities
Family	Revenue and Taxation
Financial	Streets and Highways
Fish and Game	Unemployment Insurance
Food and Agriculture	Vehicle
Government	Water
Harbors and Navigation	Welfare and Institutions
Health and Safety	

codes is then divided into sections. For example, California Penal Code §451 states what constitutes arson. The citation to this statute is Cal. Penal Code §451. Note that California lawyers refer to Cal. Penal Code §451 as both a "statute" and a "code section."

Within various codes, sections may be grouped according to subtopics, though all the codes do not use the same divisions. To continue the arson example, in the Penal Code, Title 13 addresses crimes against property, Chapter 1 concerns the crime of arson, and section 451 states what constitutes arson. Subdivisions of a section are indicated by (a), (b), (c), etc. Subdivision (a) of §451 provides punishment of up to nine years in prison for arson that causes great bodily injury. The citation to this subdivision is Cal. Penal Code §451(a). Be careful because older statutes may include a letter without parentheses, such as §403a, which should not be confused with subdivision (a) of a different §403, which is written as §403(a).

B. The Research Process in Print Codes

How you begin the process of researching in California statutes depends on what information you have before you start. If you know which statute controls your situation, you can go directly to the volumes on the shelf. The name of each code is printed on the spine of the volume or volumes that contain that code. For example, "Health and Safety" and "Penal" are listed on the spines of the books, and the codes are shelved in alphabetical order. Simply find the appropriate code and then look at the section numbers listed on the spine of each volume for that code. Page through the relevant volume to find the statute's section number.

More often, you will begin research knowing only the client's facts. In that situation, follow the outline given in Table 6-1 at the beginning of this chapter, which is explained below.

1. Search the Index for Research Terms

Take your research terms to the General Index volumes shelved at the end of either *Deering's California Codes Annotated* or *West's Annotated California Codes*. Search for every one of your research terms and write down all the statutory references given. Do not stop reviewing the index after finding just one or two statute references; several statutes may address your issue. Note that "et seq." refers to the section listed and the sections that follow it. Sometimes a research term will be included in the index but will be followed by a cross-reference to another index term. Referring to that term may lead you to other relevant statutes. See Figure 6-1 for an example of an index section.

Figure 6-1. Selected Entries for ARSON in *Deering's* Index

ARSON, Pen §§ 450 to 457.1
Attempts, Pen § 455
Forests fires, PubRes § 4418
Inhabited structures or property, Pen §§ 451, 452
Pecuniary motives, Pen § 456
Solicitation, Pen § 653f

Source: *Deering's California Codes Annotated, Index*, page 126 (2007). Reproduced with permission of LexisNexis Matthew Bender. Further reproduction of any kind is strictly prohibited.

2. Find and Read the Statutory Language

Both *Deering's* and *West's* contain the text of each statute, arranged in numerical order. For each statutory citation you found in the General Index, select the volume that contains the code name and section number in the citation, and then find the statute itself. Because the print volumes are not republished every year, the publishers include a pocket part or paperbound supplement that includes new statutes enacted since the bound volume was published, as well as additions to and deletions from statutes in the bound volume. Check the pocket part to see if the language of the statute has changed since the hardbound volume was published. Both *Deering's* and *West's* reprint the entire statutory section in the pocket part if the statute has been amended. *Deering's* indicates additions and changes by using italics and indicates deletions by inserting asterisks, while *West's* indicates additions and changes by underlining and indicates deletions by inserting asterisks. If the hardbound volume is particularly old, the pocket part may be too large to fit in the pocket and will be replaced by a separate softbound volume, which should be shelved next to the hardbound volume. Failing to check the pocket part or softbound volume can be a serious error, so be sure to do it before you do anything else.

Next, read the statute very carefully, in both the main volume and the pocket part. Statutes are the product of legislative compromises and negotiations, so their language is often not clear enough to convey all possible meanings on one reading. Therefore, careful research

Figure 6-2. Example California Code Section

---

§ 451. **Arson of structure, forest land or property; great bodily injury; inhabited structure or property; owned property; punishment.**

A person is guilty of arson when he or she willfully and maliciously sets fire to or burns or causes to be burned or who aids, counsels, or procures the burning of, any structure, forest land, or property.

(a) Arson that causes great bodily injury is a felony punishable by imprisonment in the state prison for five, seven, or nine years.

(b) Arson that causes an inhabited structure or inhabited property to burn is a felony punishable by imprisonment in the state prison for three, five, or eight years.

(c) Arson of a structure or forest land is a felony punishable by imprisonment in the state prison for two, four, or six years.

Source: *West's Annotated California Codes*, Penal Code sections 319 to 593g, page 298 (1999). Reprinted with permission of Thomson Reuters.

may require multiple readings of the statutory language before you can fully understand its meaning and legal relevance.

Moreover, you may need to read more than one code section and even other, related code sections. One section may contain general provisions, while others contain definitions and exceptions. The example code section in Figure 6-2 provides a definition of the crime of arson and indicates the possible punishments, depending on what kind of property was burned and whether anyone was injured. However, to know if your client acted "maliciously," you would have to look at section 450 of the Penal Code, which defines the term.

To ensure that you understand the statute, break it into its elements. Using bullet points or an outline format is helpful for identifying the individual elements. Connecting words and punctuation may help delineate the relationships between the various elements. For example, "and" means that all the elements must be present for the statute to apply, while "or" means that only one of the elements connected by "or" needs to be present. Table 6-3 breaks the first part of California Penal Code § 451 into its elements. Note that the bold words following the section number in Figure 6-2 are not part of the statutory language and should be not included in your

Table 6-3. Elements of Arson

- a person is guilty of arson who
  - -willfully <u>and</u> maliciously
- acts by
  - -setting fire to
  - -burning
  - -causing to be burned <u>or</u>
  - -aiding, counseling, or procuring the burning of
- any
  - -structure
  - -forest land <u>or</u>
  - -property

---

outline. These words have been supplied by the publisher, and they are not identical in *Deering's* and *West's*.

3. Find Cases that Interpret or Apply the Statute

Legislatures write statutes to apply to a wide variety of factual situations, so they are intentionally broad and often vague or ambiguous. Unless the relevant statute is very recent, it likely has been interpreted by courts. The resulting judicial opinions will help you determine if and how the statute applies to your client's specific facts.

Both *Deering's* and *West's* annotated codes contain annotations to cases that have interpreted each code section. In *West's*, the annotations are the same case annotations used in the headnotes of cases in West reporters and in West digests (discussed in Chapters 3 and 4). The annotations in *Deering's* are written by its publisher, LexisNexis, so their wording differs from the wording in the annotations written by West. However, the concept is the same in both instances.

These annotations are divided topically. For instance, in addition to looking at the subdivision of the arson statute that defines "maliciously," you can also find annotations that interpret that term. You can also find cases that interpret terms not defined in the statute, such as "burning." If the hardbound volume has a pocket part or supplement, it may contain annotations to more recent cases.

The editorial material in both code sets includes other research aids such as cross-references to other statutes that relate to the arson statute, law review and other journal articles about the substance or application of the statute, and references to other publications produced by the publisher. Since the two annotated codes have different publishers, they may refer to different law review and journal articles, and the references to other publications are different in each set. However, regardless of the annotated code you use, the case notes and the references to other statutes and publications provide an extremely helpful starting point for researching any problem involving this particular statute.

C. Other Helpful Features of Print Annotated Codes

In both *Deering's* and *West's*, immediately following the text of the statute you will find in parentheses the enactment and amendment history of the section. This history shows when the statute was first enacted, and the years, session law numbers, and effective date for each amendment in chronological order. Thus, the most recent amendment will be listed last. Under this parenthetical, the publisher also includes notes detailing the changes made by each amendment. These histories are extremely useful because a statute can be enforced only if it was in effect at the time of the event on which the criminal charge or civil suit is based. You should read these sections carefully to make sure that the statute actually applies to your client's situation.

II. Researching California Statutes Online

A. Beginning with a Statutory Citation

Researching California statutes online can be one of the most difficult forms of online research unless you have the citation to the appropriate statute. You can retrieve a statute whose citation you know by using the "Get a Document" feature on Lexis.com or by typing the citation into the search box on Lexis Advance. On Westlaw Classic you can use the "Find by citation" feature, and on West-lawNext you can type the citation into the search box, making sure that the jurisdiction box says "California." You will not need to check for more recent statutory language in a pocket part or supplement, of course, because online services are updated almost immediately when statutory language changes.

Once you have the relevant statutory section, both systems allow you to move to adjacent sections so that you can see the entire statute. On Lexis.com, click on "Book Browse" and then click on the arrows alongside the statutory code name and section number; on Lexis Advance, click on the "Previous" or "Next" arrows at the top left and right corners of the screen. On Westlaw Classic, there is no need to move into a different format; just click on "Previous Section" or "Next Section" alongside the code name and section number on the screen in which the statute first appears. On WestlawNext, look above the text of the statute and find a section symbol with a green arrow on either side. You can also click on the "Table of Contents" tab to the right of the section symbol and green arrows to get a pop-up window with the table of contents for the code.

B. Beginning without a Statutory Citation

If you do not have a citation to the statute, online statutory research is more difficult. The California codes are long, and many statutes share the same language. In addition, any time that an annotation quotes the language of a statute, an online search will pick up that language.[3] Finally, as noted above, statutes are often written using very general language, which means that the same general language may turn up in statutes having very different subject matters. Nevertheless, if you need to do statutory research online, either be-

---

3. One way to eliminate the problem of getting results based on the annotations is to start by searching online in the unannotated version of the code, for example on Lexis.com or Westlaw Classic. Once that search identifies the appropriate statute, you can continue your research as discussed immediately above in "Beginning with a Statutory Citation."

cause you prefer online research or because print sources are un-available, follow the steps outlined in Table 6-4.

In addition to Lexis and Westlaw, you can also find California statutes in several free online sources. However, these sites will give you the statutory language only; to get the annotations to cases that have interpreted and applied the statute or references to secondary sources that have discussed the statute, you must use one of the fee-based systems.

The State of California provides a searchable database for statutes at http://leginfo.legislature.ca.gov. To find the relevant statute, it is best, however, to know the name of the code you want to search. You can do either a "code search" or a "text search." For the Code Search, click on the list of Codes and enter the number of the Code section to retrieve the section directly. For a Text Search, check the box for the relevant Code and enter the search term or terms in the box. The results of the search appear in groups of ten; the Code section you want may well not be in the first group that comes up. You can also access this site through various law library sites, such as that of the Law Library of Congress at www.loc.gov/law/help/guide.pho, which provides access to the statutes of all states and of the federal government. As with other free systems, these databases include only the text of the statutes with no case references or other editorial aids.

III. Applying and Interpreting California Statutes

In general, applying a statute means (1) reading its words carefully, (2) understanding its elements, (3) reading any related or referenced statutes, (4) analyzing cases that apply or interpret the statutes, and (5) applying the law to the facts of your client's case. In the fourth step, you will sometimes need to consider *how* the California courts interpret statutory language

Fundamentally, California courts seek to "ascertain and effectuate legislative intent."[4] "An equally basic rule of statutory construction, however, is that courts are bound to give effect to statutes according to the usual, ordinary import of the language employed in

---

4. *Kimmel v. Goland*, 51 Cal. 3d 202, 208 (1990).

Table 6-4. Researching California Statutes Online

Lexis.com	Westlaw Classic
1. On the home page click on "States-Legal — U.S." and choose "California"	1. Choose "Directory" at the top, then "U.S. State Materials"; choose "California"
2. Choose "CA—Deering's California Codes Annotated"	2. Click on "Statutes & Legislative Materials"
3. Enter a terms-and-connectors or natural-language search or narrow the search by clicking on specific titles	3. Click on California Statutes-Annotated
	4. Enter a terms-and-connectors or natural-language search
4. Narrow the results by using "Focus"	5. Narrow the results by entering terms in the "Locate" box
5. Choose from among the resulting cites	6. Choose from among the resulting cites

Lexis Advance	WestlawNext
1. Choose "Statutes and Legislation" in the content box below the main search box	1. Click on "State Materials" below the "Browse" heading
2. Choose "California" in the jurisdiction box below the main search box	2. Choose "California"
	3. Click on "California Statutes and Court Rules"
3. Enter search terms in the search box	4. Enter search terms in the search box
4. Narrow the results by entering further terms-and-connectors words in the "Search within results" box	5. Narrow the results by applying filters in the left margin: search within results; effective date; or statute title
5. Choose from among the resulting cites	6. Choose from among the resulting cites

framing them."[5] In other words, courts should apply the plain meaning of the words. The court should, where possible, look at every word and phrase, and should avoid a construction that makes language superfluous.[6] In addition, the words should be construed in context with the statutory purpose and the entire statutory framework in mind.[7] Finally, the statute should be interpreted, if possible, in harmony with any applicable constitutional provisions.[8] If the words of the statute are clear and unambiguous, the court should not look to any extrinsic aids to determine the legislature's intent. However, if more than one construction of the language is reasonable, the court may look to legislative history to ascertain legislative intent.[9]

Thus, you should look at the words of the statute to see if they are clear and unambiguous. If they are, you should apply their plain meaning to your analysis of how the statute applies. If they are ambiguous in the sense of there being more than one reasonable interpretation, turn to legislative history, discussed in Chapter 7.[10]

As you begin to understand the statute and develop your analysis, follow these guidelines in drafting your document:

- Quote the relevant portion of the statute in enough detail to provide context without overwhelming your reader with unnecessary language.

- Omit parts of the statute that do not apply to your facts.

- Paraphrase parts of the statute that are difficult for your reader to understand and are not critical to your analysis.

---

5. *Cal. Teachers Ass'n v. San Diego Community College Dist.*, 28 Cal. 3d 692, 698 (1981).

6. *Moyer v. Workmen's Compen. Apps. Bd.*, 10 Cal. 3d 222, 230 (1973).

7. *Id.*

8. *In re Marquez*, 30 Cal. 4th 14, 20 (2003).

9. *People v. Robles*, 23 Cal. 4th 1106, 1111 (2000).

10. As an advocate, it is often necessary to explore legislative history even if you think the statute is unambiguous because lawyers often make arguments in the alternative (e.g., the statute is clear, but even if the court finds otherwise, the legislative history also supports your client's interpretation of the statute).

If quoting requires you to use many ellipses to indicate omitted language, it may be better to paraphrase. But be careful not to change the meaning of the statutory language.

IV. Researching the Statutes of Other States

Every state has codified statutes, but the names vary from state to state. Examples include *Hawaii Revised Statutes*, *Pennsylvania Consolidated Statutes*, and *South Dakota Codified Laws*. A national citation manual will list the name of the statutory code for each state; alternatively, a quick Google search will retrieve the state legislature's website, with references to its code.

While the same basic process applies to statutory research in other states, there may be some important differences. California is unusual in having both a subject name and a section number; only New York and Texas follow this pattern. Most states number their statutes using a combination of numerals and decimal points, although not all states use the same numbering system. For example, the following citations all indicate a statutory section of definitions relating to arson: Ariz. Rev. Stat. Ann. § 13-1701 (Arizona); Nev. Rev. Stat. § 205.005 (Nevada); Or. Rev. Stat. § 164.305 (Oregon); and Wash. Rev. Code § 9A.48.010 (Washington).

V. Researching Federal Statutes

The official text of federal statutes is published in *United States Code* (U.S.C.). Similar to the organization of California statutes, federal statutes are codified under subject-matter titles, each of which is numbered. There are fifty-one titles in U.S.C., and each title is further subdivided into section numbers. To cite a federal statute, you must include the number of the title and the number of the specific section. For example, the statute under which the Environmental Protection Agency regulates emission standards for new cars is 42 U.S.C.

§ 7521 (2006). Title 42 is devoted to Public Health and Welfare, and 7521 is the specific section in the Clean Air Act that is assigned to new car emission standards. That volume of U.S.C. was published in 2006.

U.S.C. is updated infrequently and does not include any annotations or other editorial research aids, so it has very limited research value. The absence of annotations and other editorial aids also limits the usefulness of the online sites maintained by the federal government, such as the Federal Digital System at www.gpo.gov/fdsys. The sources you are more likely to use are *United States Code Annotated* (U.S.C.A.) and *United States Code Service* (U.S.C.S.), published by West and LexisNexis, respectively. In print, U.S.C.A. and U.S.C.S. are updated through pocket parts and softbound supplements. These annotated codes can also be found online through Westlaw and Lexis, where they are updated frequently. If the current text of the statute is not available in U.S.C., however, citing U.S.C.A. or U.S.C.S. in print may be preferred over citing an online code.

Both U.S.C.A. and U.S.C.S. — in print and online — contain the text of federal statutes, references to related research sources, and annotations that refer to cases interpreting or applying the statute. While attorneys and librarians have their preferences between the two, U.S.C.A. and U.S.C.S. are virtually interchangeable, and in practice you should simply use whichever one you have access to.

Both annotated federal codes contain information other than statutes and research annotations. For example, they provide references to federal regulations and executive orders. (See Chapter 8 for a discussion of administrative law.) Both U.S.C.S. and U.S.C.A. include tables listing statutes by their popular names; these are available on Lexis and Westlaw, too. Finally, as explained in the next part, both contain federal court rules.

VI. Researching Court Rules

Court rules are frequently published in statutory codifications, and both of California's annotated codes do so. Court rules govern litigation practice from the filing of initial pleadings through the final appeal. Rules dictate litigation details ranging from the correct caption for pleadings to the rules of procedure for the probate courts and rules on both civil and criminal appeals. Ethical rules may also govern who can practice law in the state, including rules about disciplinary proceedings and legal education.[11]

Court rules are primary authority, even though the court or legislature responsible for them has delegated rule-making power to a council, committee, or other body. Complying with these rules is essential for success in any litigation. Rules are written in outline form like statutes, and techniques for reading and applying statutes apply equally to rules: read each word of a rule carefully, outline complicated provisions, refer to cross-referenced rules, and scan other rules nearby to see whether they are related.

A. California Court Rules

The Judicial Council of California is the policy-making body for courts of California.[12] It has adopted California's Rules of Court, which apply to all courts in the state. Both *Deering's California Codes Annotated* and *West's Annotated California Codes* publish multiple volumes of California court rules. In *Deering's*, they appear under the title "Rules of Court," while in *West's* they are under "Court Rules." However, the rules included are the same. In addition, both publishers include State Bar Rules in the last volume of the court rules. These rules relate to the California State Bar, its members, programs, and relationships with other entities. As with California statutes, the Rules of Court and the State Bar Rules are available electronically on Lexis and Westlaw services.

The California Rules of Court were divided into ten titles following a reorganization adopted by the Judicial Council in 2006 (see Table 6-5). The reorganization repealed former rules, added new rules, and renumbered existing rules. Because of this reorganization,

---

11. Title 9, Chapter 2 of the California Rules of Court covers Attorney Disciplinary Proceedings, and Chapter 3 covers Legal Education.

12. *See* www.courts.ca.gov/policyadmin-jc.htm.

Table 6-5. California Rules of Court

Title 1	Rules Applicable to all Courts
Title 2	Trial Court Rules
Title 3	Civil Rules
Title 4	Criminal Rules
Title 5	Family and Juvenile Rules
Title 6	[Reserved]
Title 7	Probate Rules
Title 8	Appellate Rules
Title 9	Rules on Law Practice, Attorneys, and Judges
Title 10	Judicial Administration Rules

you will need to use a Derivation Table created by the Judicial Council to translate the old rule numbers into the new rule numbers.[13]

The numbering system for the reorganized rules consists of two numbers separated by a decimal point. The first number, a number between one and ten, reflects the title. The number following the decimal point is a one-, two-, three-, or four-digit number, and these numbers rise progressively through the title. (See Figure 6-3.) Thus, to find a particular rule when you know its number, look in the correct title as indicated by the first number, and then look to the numbers after the decimal point.

The California Rules of Court are also available online at www.courts.ca.gov/rules.htm. You can use the same site to find local rules, additional rules enacted by each superior court that govern practice in that court. Although both *Deering's* and *West's* update their print volumes with pocket parts, because the rules change fre-

---

13. For example, the rule governing sanctions for violation of the court rules for civil proceedings, formerly Rule 227, is now Rule 2.30 in the reorganized Rules of Court. This derivation table is printed in both *Deering's* and *West's* in the beginning of the first volume of court rules.

Figure 6-3. Numbering of California Court Rules

California
Rules of
Court
(Revised
January 1,
2013)

Print this page

Close this window
when you finish printing

Title 2. Trial Court Rules

Division 1. General Provisions
Chapter 1. Title and Application
    Rule 2.1. Title
    Rule 2.2. Application
Chapter 2. Definitions and Scope of Rules
    Rule 2.3. Definitions
    Rule 2.10. Scope of rules [Reserved]
Chapter 3. Timing
    Rule 2.20. Application for an order extending time
Chapter 4. Sanctions
    Rule 2.30. Sanctions for rules violations in civil cases
Division 2. Papers and Forms to Be Filed
Chapter 1. Papers
    Rule 2.100. Form and format of papers presented for filing in the trial courts
    Rule 2.101. Use of recycled paper; certification by attorney or party
    Rule 2.102. One-sided paper
    Rule 2.103. Quality, color, and size of paper

Source: California Rules of Court on California Courts website, www.courts.ca.gov/cms/rules/index.cfm?title=two.

quently, this site is the best source for the rules. Click on the "Local Rules" link to reach a menu of rules for each superior court, organized by county. When practicing in any superior court in California, therefore, you must check both the California Rules of Court and the local rules to be sure your filings are technically correct.

As with the other volumes in the series, the publishers in both *Deering's* and *West's* have included annotations to cases that have applied the rule or its predecessor rule. *West's* includes an "Advisory Committee Comment" when one is available following the text of the rule, while *Deering's* puts these comments in footnotes. The comments are similar to legislative history for the rule and are persuasive authority only.[14]

Finally, both *Deering's* and *West's* publish softbound volumes of California Judicial Council forms. These forms are for use in the courts, and they cover a vast array of pleadings and other court forms. The forms are also available online at www.courts.ca.gov/forms.htm in PDF format.

B. Federal Court Rules

Court rules exist on the federal level as well. They are published in U.S.C., U.S.C.A., and U.S.C.S.,[15] and by the individual federal courts. Federal rules are available on Lexis, Westlaw, and various court websites.

As at the state level, each court may also have its own rules that either replace or supplement the general federal court rules. Thus, for example, the rules of the Eastern District of California may vary considerably from the rules of the neighboring Northern District of California. The easiest way to find these federal district court rules is on the website of the U.S. courts at www.uscourts.gov/RulesandPolicies.aspx.

Cases relevant to federal rules can be located using the annotated codes or with the techniques for case research explained in Chapter 4. In addition, *Federal Practice Digest*, *Federal Rules Service* (rules of procedure), and *Federal Rules of Evidence Service* may be useful tools. Treatises on federal rules are covered in Chapter 10, Part IV.B.

---

14. Advisory committees advise the Judicial Council "in studying the condition of court business, improving judicial administration, and performing other council responsibilities." Members of advisory committees are appointed by the Chief Justice of the Supreme Court as chair of the Judicial Council from judges, court officials, lawyers, and members of the public. *See* www.courts.ca.gov/policyadmin-jc.htm.

15. Placement of the rules varies among the print statutory publications. In U.S.C. and U.S.C.A., for example, the Federal Rules of Appellate Procedure appear just after Title 28, whose topic is "Judiciary and Judicial Procedure." In U.S.C.S., those rules are found at the end of all titles in separate volumes devoted to rules.

Chapter 7

Legislative History

Legislative history is the term used to describe the documents produced or considered by the California Legislature during the legislative process. These documents may help explain the intent of the legislature—why the legislature wrote the law in the way that it did. Legislative history research is most often relevant in litigation when a lawyer needs to convince a court to interpret a statute in a way that is favorable to a client's position.[1] And when pending legislation may affect a client, a lawyer may need to engage in bill tracking—the monitoring of current bills that may or may not ultimately become law.

This chapter begins with an overview of the legislative process in California, including a discussion of the documents produced by the California Legislature during that process. Understanding the legislative process is important in making a legislative intent argument because finding the legislature's intent in passing a statute may require the following types of analysis: (a) comparing various iterations of the bill that was eventually enacted into law, (b) reading statements by key legislators during the legislative debate over the bill, and (c) considering the official of bill analyses by the legislature's professional committee staff.

Next, the chapter explains how these legislative documents are helpful in bill tracking. The chapter then explains how to use these and other documents to research the legislative history of a statute. Because legislation in California can also come directly from the peo-

---

1. In fact, the California Code of Civil Procedure requires that when a court construes a statute, it must determine the intent of the legislature if possible. Cal. Civ. Proc. Code Ann. § 1859 (West 2007).

ple in the form of a ballot initiative, the chapter also explains the initiative and referendum process, including how to research the legislative history of laws that are adopted directly by the voters. The chapter concludes with a brief overview of research involving the federal legislative process.

I. The Legislative Process in California

The California Legislature contains two houses, the Senate and the Assembly.[2] The California Senate has forty members who serve four-year terms, and the Assembly has eighty members who serve two-year terms.[3] Each house has its own website. The Senate's is senate.ca.gov, and the Assembly's is assembly.ca.gov. Both provide information about legislators, pending legislation, committees, and other legislative matters. A separate site is maintained by the Office of Legislative Counsel, a nonpartisan public agency that serves as counsel to the legislature.[4] The Legislative Counsel helps draft legislation and advises the legislature on the constitutionality and effect of proposed legislation. The Legislative Counsel's website address is legislativecounsel. ca.gov.

A legislative session in California lasts for two years. Each session begins on the first Monday in December of each even-numbered year. Sessions are numbered, however, with the odd year first and the even year second (e.g., 2013–2014).

The legislative process for enacting or amending laws in California is similar to that of other states and the federal legislature, the United States Congress. One specific requirement for all California

---

2. *See* Cal. Const. art. IV, § 1.

3. Under Proposition 28, an initiative constitutional amendment approved by the voters in 2012, legislators can serve a maximum of twelve years in either the State Senate, the State Assembly, or a combination of both houses. *See* Cal. Const. art IV, §§ 1.5 & 2.

4. The office and duties of the Legislative Counsel are statutorily defined. Cal. Gov't Code Ann. §§ 10200–10242.5 (West 2012).

statutes is that their titles must be read three times in each chamber of the legislature. Table 7-1 shows the progression of an idea from bill to statute and notes the documents generated at each step that are important in legal research. The next section of this chapter explains how to find these key legislative documents.

II. Documents Produced During the California Legislative Process

Whether you want to track the progress of a pending bill or research the history of an enacted statute, it helps to be familiar with the documents produced by the California Legislature during the legislative process. Some of these documents will be useful for bill tracking only, while others will be useful for both processes. The publications for the current year can be viewed at www.leginfo.ca.gov/legpubs.html.[5] Publications from past years can sometimes be viewed online through the Senate, Assembly, or Legislative Counsel websites, and can generally be found on microform in a library or in hard copy at the California State Archives in Sacramento.

A **Daily File** is produced by both the Assembly and the Senate. It lists current officers, the Order of Business, a tentative schedule for the entire legislative session, and a schedule of bills to be read on the floor and during committee hearings.

The **Legislative Index** is a subject-matter index of all bills being considered in the current legislative session, published by the Legislative Counsel. This index includes not only proposed statutes, but also proposed constitutional amendments, and concurrent and joint resolutions. For purposes of legislative history research, be aware that

---

5. For a detailed introduction to the legislative process in California, see Chapter 9 of *California's Legislature*, a book published by the Office of the Assembly Chief Clerk. The contents of the book can be viewed online at www.leginfo.ca.gov/legpubs.html. Click on "California's Legislature" to view the book.

Table 7-1. How a Bill Becomes a Law

Legislative Action	Documents Produced
An idea for legislation is suggested by a legislator, an agency, the governor, citizens, or lobbyists. A legislator who agrees to initiate the legislation sends the idea and proposed language to the Legislative Counsel for drafting. One or more legislators may sponsor the resulting bill.	The text of a **bill** is of paramount importance. If enacted, the bill's requirements or prohibitions may affect a client's interests. Even if a modified version is passed, comparing the original to the final version can help determine legislative intent.
The bill is introduced by a legislator in either the Senate or the Assembly. It is assigned a number, its title is read, and it is assigned to the appropriate standing committee. If the bill has a fiscal impact, it is also assigned to the Senate Appropriations Committee or the Assembly Ways and Means Committee for separate consideration. This is the first reading of the bill.	The bill is printed. The Legislative Counsel prepares a **digest** of the bill, which is printed on the first page of the bill. The **digest** summarizes the proposed changes in existing law, shows the number of votes needed to pass the bill, and indicates if the bill includes an appropriation of funds.
The committee schedules the bill for hearing. The hearing cannot occur until thirty days following the introduction and first reading, although this rule can be waived by a three-quarters vote of the house.	The **Daily File** has a schedule of committee meetings with dates that the bill is to be heard in committee. The staff of the committee prepares a **bill analysis**.
The committee holds a hearing. The bill's author presents the bill to the committee. Testimony may be taken in support or opposition.	Committee meetings are open to the public, but no record is required to be made and hearings of standing committees are almost never published. (They may be recorded and may be available in the archives of the California Channel.)
The committee votes on the bill, and the chair of the committee reports the committee recommendation to that house. The committee recommendation may be: Do pass; Do pass, as amended; or Be amended.	The committee vote is recorded and published in the *Journal* of that house. The committee's recommendation is reported in the *Journal* and the **Daily History**.
If the bill is passed by the committee, it is read a second time in the house of origin and placed "on file" for the third reading.	The **Daily File** lists bills scheduled for second reading. If the bill was reported out of committee with amendments and these amendments are adopted on the floor of that house, the bill is **reprinted**. The Legislative Counsel's **digest** is revised each time the bill is amended to reflect the resulting changes.

Table 7-1. How a Bill Becomes a Law, *continued*

Legislative Action	Documents Produced
The bill is read a third time in the house of origin, explained by the author, discussed in that house, and voted on by roll call vote.	Debates are not published. *Journals* provide a record of the proceedings. However, they record only the votes.
Once the bill is approved by the house of origin, it goes to the second house, where the same process of consideration is repeated. There are three routes for the bill to become law: approval by the second house in the same form; approval by the second house in amended form, which the first house accepts; or approval by the second house in amended form that the first house rejects, resulting in a conference committee.	The *Journal* notes the passage of the bill and its return to the house of origin.
If the bill passes the second house, it is returned to the house of origin with a message that it was passed.	The bill is **enrolled**, meaning it is printed in its final form with blanks for signatures of legislative officers, the governor, and the secretary of state. The **digest** is omitted from this printing.
If the second house amends the bill, the house of origin must agree with the amendments, which is called concurrence.	Following **concurrence**, the bill is **enrolled**.
If the house of origin does not approve the amended version, the two houses may appoint a conference committee to draft an agreed version. If the conference committee reaches agreement, the bill is returned to both houses for a vote.	Once the agreed bill is passed by both houses, it is **enrolled**.
The enrolled bill is sent to the governor. The governor can sign the bill, let it become law without signature, or veto the bill.	The governor's action is reported in the **Daily History**.
An enacted bill is "chaptered" as a session law, meaning that it is assigned a chapter number in *Statutes and Amendments to the Codes*. Later the new statute is codified in one of California's twenty-nine codes.	A **chapter number** is merely a chronological record of when the bill was enacted. The **codification number** places the new statute with others on related topics.

if the subject of a particular bill changes during the legislative process, the original subject is not removed from the Legislative Index.[6]

The **Table of Sections Affected** is also published by the Legislative Counsel. It provides a cumulative listing of each section of the California Constitution, the codes, and uncodified laws affected by measures that are introduced in the legislature.

The Senate and the Assembly each produces a **Daily Journal.** It is the daily, official record of business that has been transacted in each house. The **Senate Daily Journal** includes the title of each measure the Senate considered, results of floor votes, messages from the governor and the Assembly, and reports from Senate committees of their deliberations on pending legislation. The **Assembly Daily Journal** shows all roll call votes, lists bill introductions, and records other official Assembly actions. At the end of the session, each *Journal* is bound in book form.

Each house produces a **Daily History** at the end of each day's session. The Daily History lists specific actions taken on legislation, listed in numerical order. At the end of the week, the Daily History is accumulated into a **Weekly History.** Similarly, at the end of the legislative session, the Weekly Histories are compiled into a **Final History** that shows the disposition of all measures introduced during that session.[7]

---

6. Members of the legislature may introduce only a limited number of bills in the course of a single session and must introduce most of them before the end of February. *See* California Legislature Jt. R. 54, at www.leginfo.ca.gov/rules/joint_rules.pdf. To preserve the opportunity to introduce legislation on a particular topic after the February deadline, legislators often introduce bills with "dummy" subjects, which are then entered in the index. When the bill is amended to change the subject completely, the original "dummy" subject remains in the index.

7. Final Histories for both the Senate and the Assembly and *Journals* of each house for many of the years between 1849 and 2008 can be found online at http://192.234.213.35/clerkarchive. Click "Sessions of the California Legislature from 1849–2008" to view the PDf chart. Both Final Histories and *Journals* may be available in your library in print.

III. California Bill Tracking

Each year, California legislators introduce a large number of bills that may or may not be enacted into law. These bills may affect the rights of a client by proposing new laws or amending existing laws. To properly advise a client, an attorney needs to identify new bills that could affect the client's interests and follow their progress through the legislative process. This bill tracking can be done online through the official site for California legislative information that is maintained by the Legislative Counsel or using other resources, as discussed below.

A. Legislative Counsel Resources

The Legislative Counsel's website allows you to search for legislation from 1993 through the present legislative session using the bill number, the author of the bill, or key words that appear in the bill.

For example, if you know the number of a bill, you can track it by going to the section of the Legislative Counsel's website devoted to California legislative information. Historically, that web address has been www.leginfo.ca.gov, but current legislative information is now also available at http://leginfo.legislature.ca.gov.[8] Using either web address, you can access information about a particular bill by clicking on "Bill Information."[9] You can search on the "Bill Information" page by bill number, author, or key word. If you know whether the bill originated in the Senate or the Assembly, you can choose to search

---

8. Both websites are administered by the Legislative Counsel's office. The traditional site, www.leginfo.ca.gov, has legislative information from 1993 to the present. The new website, http://leginfo.legislature.ca.gov, has additional features but only has legislative information from 1999 to the present.

9. Similar searches can be conducted on the Senate and Assembly websites, senate.ca.gov and assembly.ca.gov, from the "Legislation" links.

only in the house of origin. Otherwise, you can search in both houses. Simply click on "Bill Number," enter the number in the box, and click on "Search."

The resulting listing will include every bill with that number, and may include the following types of bills: Assembly Bill (AB), Assembly Constitutional Amendment (ACA), Assembly Joint Resolution (AJR), House Resolution (HR), Senate Bill (SB), Senate Constitutional Amendment (SCA), Senate Concurrent Resolution (SCR), Senate Joint Resolution (SJR), or Senate Resolution (SR).[10] For example, if the bill you are tracking is Assembly Bill 33, typing "33" into the query box will bring up all bills with the number "33." Simply click on the link for a particular bill to get a listing of all documents associated with it.

If you do not know the bill number, you can search on the same pages of the Legislative Counsel's website by author or by key word. From the "Bill Information" page, typing in either the author or the key words of the bill title will lead you to a list of bills to choose from.

Once you locate the bill that you are tracking, you can sign up through the Legislative Counsel's website to receive an email update whenever the legislature takes significant action on the bill.

B. Other Approaches to Bill Tracking

While the Legislative Counsel's website is often the easiest way to track a bill, there are other options as well.

You can also track a pending bill by consulting the Daily File for both houses, which you can access either through the Legislative Counsel's website or through the websites for both houses.[11]

---

10. According to the Joint Rules of the Senate and Assembly, the term "bills" includes house, concurrent, and joint resolutions and constitutional amendments, as well as proposed legislation. E. Dotson Wilson & Brian S. Ebbert, *California's Legislature* 110 (Office of the Assembly Chief Clerk 2006) (available at www.leginfo.ca.gov/pdf/Ch_09_CaLegi06.pdf).

11. To access the Daily File through the Legislative Counsel's website, go to www.leginfo.ca.gov, click on the hyperlink for "Legislative WWW Sites," click on either "California Assembley" or "California Senate," and then click on "Daily File." To access the Daily File through the websites for both houses

Another approach is to consult the Legislative Index, at www.leginfo.ca.gov/legpubs.html, which was mentioned earlier in this chapter. This index is organized by subject matter as well as by bill author and is published by the Legislative Counsel. However, as noted above, this index does not indicate when subject matter is removed from a bill during the legislative process. The Legislative Counsel also provides a Table of Sections Affected, which you can use to see if existing statutes relating to your client's interests will potentially be affected by pending legislation. The index is available in California depository libraries and is sold in Sacramento by the Legislative Bill Room.

Another possible way to track pending legislation is by listening to audio recordings or watching video broadcasts of legislative sessions or committee hearings. For the most part, the Assembly audiotapes only, while the Senate both audio and video records some sessions and committee hearings. Notice of recorded hearings can be found on both the Senate and the Assembly websites, and many Senate and some Assembly hearings are available on the California Channel; check the California Channel website at www.calchannel.com.

You can keep up with newly enacted legislation in print sources by consulting either *Deering's Advance Legislative Service* or *West's California Legislative Service*. Both of these services consist of softbound pamphlets that are published at regular intervals throughout the year. They include both chaptered laws (enacted laws that have not yet been inserted in the codes) and state court rule amendments, as well as lists of code sections affected by new legislation. *West's California Legislative Service* also includes proposed constitutional amendments and ballot propositions.

Finally, you can contact the office of a member of the State Assembly or State Senate for assistance in bill tracking. The office of the member of the legislature who authored the bill you are tracking is most likely to be able to assist you in learning about the bill's status.

---

directly, visit either senate.ca.gov or assembly.ca.gov, click on "Schedules and Publications" and then click on "Daily File."

IV. California Legislative History Research

A. In General

Lawyers conduct legislative history research to shed light on the meaning of a statute. Legislative history research is especially useful for legislation that has not yet been interpreted by the courts. Especially when the text of a statute is ambiguous, reviewing the documents created in the course of enacting the statute can assist in determining the legislature's intent. When litigation involves a statute whose meaning is arguably unclear, first look to see if courts have definitively interpreted the statute. If not, you will need to turn to legislative history and refer to it in your briefs to the court.[12]

Legislative history research is the reverse of bill tracking. Bill tracking follows the legislative process forward from the introduction of a bill; legislative history research follows the legislative process backward from the enacted statute. Therefore, many of the sources you would consult in their current editions for bill tracking will also be necessary for legislative history research, but this time for past years. From the statute as it appears in either *Deering's California Codes Annotated* or *West's Annotated California Codes*, you can follow the statute's legislative history through the session law chapter number, then the bill number, and finally the documents produced by the legislative process.

This section explains the sources of legislative history in California and how to conduct legislative history research. Some information is available locally in print and microfilm, and most information for statutes passed after January 1, 1993, is available online through the Legislative Counsel's website. For some statutes, however, you will

---

12. Remember that you need to provide the court with a copy of any legislative history materials on which you rely in a brief. Legislative history materials are often submitted to the court through a request for judicial notice. *See Kaufman & Broad Communities, Inc. v. Performance Plastering, Inc.*, 133 Cal. App. 4th 26, 29–31 (3d Dist. 2005) (discussing protocol for submitting legislative history materials via request for judicial notice).

need to contact the California State Archives in Sacramento[13] or check with the Chief Clerk of the State Assembly or the California State Library, also in Sacramento.

The California State Archives, in particular, can be a helpful source of legislative history for statutes passed between 1943 and 1993. It is not necessary to travel to Sacramento to use the Archives' resources. Once you have identified the original bill number and year of the statute (as explained below), you can contact the Archives by telephone and request a copy of the "legislative bill files" for that bill. For a nominal per-page copying charge and mailing fee, the Archives will locate, copy, and mail the bill files to you.

As an alternative, practicing attorneys may instead rely on commercial services that conduct legislative history research for a fee.[14]

B. Researching the Legislative History of a California Statute

Table 7-2 outlines the steps needed to research the legislative history of a California statute. As an example, suppose you have learned of a statute that assesses a fine for leaving a child six years old or younger unsupervised in a car under certain circumstances. The statute is codified at Cal. Veh. Code § 15620. The statutory language says that those circumstances include "conditions that present a significant risk to the child's health or safety," but it does not define what those conditions are. It is possible that researching the legislative history of the statute will give you more information.

---

13. The California State Archives' website is located at www.sos.ca.gov/archives/.

14. The leading commercial services are Legislative Intent Service, www.legintent.com; Legislative Research & Intent LLC, www.lrihistory.com; and Legislative History & Intent, www.legislativeintent.com.

Table 7-2. Outline for Legislative History Research in California

1. Review the history note following a published statute to learn the original bill number.
2. Gather background information by locating the citation to the statute in *Statutes and Amendments to the Codes*.
3. Read the Legislative Counsel's Digest, printed at the beginning of the session law.
4. Review the text of the bill and all proposed amendments to the original text.
5. Read any available committee staff Bill Analyses.
6. Read the Legislative Counsel Opinion, if one is available.
7. Look at Letters of Intent, if available.
8. Read the Governor's Signing Statement, if available.
9. Read any relevant material in the "Review of Selected California Legislation," published by the *McGeorge Law Review*.

1. Find the Original Bill Number

Legislative history research starts with the enacted statute, which can be found in both *West's Annotated California Codes* and *Deering's California Codes Annotated* and online through Lexis or Westlaw. At the end of the statutory language, the publisher provides a note that gives the history of the statute. Often the note is placed in brackets or parentheses to distinguish it from the text of the statute. This note includes a reference to the chaptered session law number, the date for the code section, and the original bill number. The original bill number for Cal. Veh. Code § 15620 was SB 255; it was enacted in 2001.

The note will also include a reference to any amendments to the statute since it was first enacted. For example, Cal. Veh. Code § 15620 was amended via AB 3034 in 2002. It may be necessary to review the original language of the statute as well as the amended statute to determine when the language you are trying to interpret was added to the statute. In this example, the phrase "conditions that present a significant risk to the child's health or safety" was in the original statute that was enacted in 2001. So the legislative history of SB 255 from 2001 will be most relevant to your analysis. But if the legislature had added that language to the statute in 2002, you would instead want to locate the legislative history of AB 3034 from 2002.

2. Gather Session Law Information

The next step is to find the appropriate volume of *Statutes and Amendments to the Codes*,[15] the compilation of all "chaptered" bills enacted in each two-year session of the legislature. A bill is "chaptered" after it has been enacted and is sent to the secretary of state's office; these compiled enacted laws are called "session laws." Session laws print statutes in the form in which they were enacted by the legislature and in the chronological order in which they were enacted. Each new law is assigned a "chapter" number, which simply indicates the chronological order in which it was enacted. Either use the bill number you found in the annotated code, or search the Table of Laws Enacted in volume 1 of *Statutes and Amendments to the Codes* for that year or the Summary Digest in the final volume for the year to find the bill number.

3. Read the Legislative Counsel's Digest

At the beginning of the session law, you will see the bill digest. The Legislative Counsel creates the digest and attaches it to each bill when it is first printed, immediately after the sponsor introduces the bill. The digest follows the bill through all its versions and is amended to reflect amendments to the bill. The version of the digest you see in the session law reflects the final text of the statute. Before 1999, this digest tended merely to list other code sections affected by this bill. Since 1999, the digest has become more descriptive of the contents and purpose of the bill, so more recent digests will be much more useful for legislative history research.

The session law may also include uncodified legislative intent language that does not become part of the statute itself. In the case of

---

15. Both the *ALWD Manual* and the *Bluebook* refer to this publication as *Statutes of California*, but the text itself and California librarians refer to it as *Statutes and Amendments to the Codes*.

SB 255, which became Cal. Veh. Code § 15620, the uncodified language tells you that the legislature was concerned about a "child's access to the vehicle's controls" and the "exposure of the child to extreme cold or heat." These concerns can be useful to you in determining the legislative intent behind this statute.[16]

4. Review the Bill's Text and Proposed Amendments

Next, review all of the versions of the bill as it passed through the legislative process. For statutes enacted after January 1, 1993, all of the versions can be found through the Legislative Counsel's website. Click on "Bill Information" and enter the legislative session by date and the bill number and click "Search." You will be able to access all versions of the bill's text from its introduction until it was chaptered, as well as the final "History" of the bill. (The final history of SB 255 is set out in Appendix 7-A of this chapter.) In looking through the versions, note that deletions are indicated by strike-outs and additions are indicated with italics. For statutes enacted before 1993, Lexis.com has the text of bills dating back to 1991. Westlaw Classic has the text of bills dating back to 2005 and has the text of chaptered laws dating back to 1987.[17] For statutes before 1987, you will have to consult microfiche in a law library or the State Archives.

5. Read the Bill Analysis

Each time a bill is considered by a Senate or Assembly committee, or is presented on the floor of either house, the staff prepares a bill analysis. These analyses can be another source of legislative intent, and you should consult them next. The bill analyses for statutes enacted after 1992 can be found on the Legislative Counsel's website or

---

16. The uncodified legislative intent language for this statute also appears in the editorial materials following the statute in *West's Annotated California Codes*. It does not appear in *Deering's California Codes Annotated*.

17. WestlawNext and Lexis Advance have some of the same bill text information as their classic counterparts but do not contain any additional information.

on Westlaw Classic; Lexis.com includes bill analyses from 1991 forward. Before that date, the only source is the State Archives.

A bill analysis includes a description of the proposed statute, its relation to existing law, actions already taken in the committee and in the other legislative house, and an analysis of the bill. The analysis may include a discussion of the author's purpose in introducing the bill and arguments in support of and opposition to the bill. It may raise issues that the staff sees presented by the text of the bill.

To continue our example, the bill analysis prepared for the Assembly Committee on Transportation noted as an area of concern in relation to Cal. Veh. Code § 15620 that the "significant risk" standard was "vague for lack of definition." (Excerpts from this analysis are provided in Appendix 7-B of this chapter.)

6. *Read Any Legislative Counsel Opinions*

Another source of legislative history is a Legislative Counsel Opinion. A legislator may ask the Legislative Counsel to interpret proposed legislation; very few bills have Legislative Counsel Opinions attached to them. *West's Annotated California Codes* prints portions of some Legislative Counsel Opinions in the editorial material immediately following the text of the statute. *Deering's California Codes Annotated* provides citations to some Legislative Counsel Opinions but does not print their text. Because neither publication includes all Legislative Counsel Opinions, it is helpful to check both. The other place to look for these opinions is in the *Journal of the Assembly* or the *Journal of the Senate*. Look in the indexes of each *Journal* under "Legislative Counsel, opinions of" or similar language. Not all Legislative Counsel Opinions are printed in the *Journals*.

7. *Other Sources for California Legislative History*

Four final sources of legislative history are important to mention here. The first is a letter of intent that the legislature may provide when it sends the bill to the governor for signing. Letters of intent may be printed in the *Journals* of the Senate or Assembly, and they may be included in the legislative bill files at the State Archives.

Second, courts sometimes consider signing statements by the governor as a possible source of legislative history. These statements may also be available in bill files at the State Archives or may be found on the governor's website at gov.ca.gov.

Third, courts sometimes consider statements of sponsors or of opponents or proponents of legislation if those statements were communicated to the entire legislative body.[18] These statements, too, may be documented in the legislative bill files at the State Archives.

Finally, one very accessible source of information about a bill's history is the annual "Review of Selected California Legislation" published by the *McGeorge Law Review* (previously the *Pacific Law Journal*) since 1970. Continuing our example, if you consulted volume 33 of the *McGeorge Law Review*, you would find that the author of SB 255 intentionally left the "significant risk" language undefined to allow police officers greater latitude when deciding if the law has been violated.[19]

With these final three sources — and with other documents beyond those mentioned here that reflect what transpired during the legislative process — it is important to consider whether the sources or documents are accepted by the courts as "as constituting cognizable legislative history."[20] For example, California courts generally do not consider statements by a bill's author to the press regarding a bill's objectives indicative of legislative intent where "there is no reliable indication that the Legislature as a whole was aware of that objective and believed the language of the proposal would accomplish it."[21] So even if you locate documents containing such statements, a California court is unlikely to rely on those documents in construing a statute.

---

18. *See e.g. In re Marriage of Siller*, 187 Cal. App. 3d 36, 46 (3d Dist. 1986) (considering floor statement of sponsoring legislator).

19. Jaeson D. White, Student Author, *Sit Right Here Honey, I'll Be Right Back: The Unattended Child in Motor Vehicle Safety Act*, 33 McGeorge L. Rev. 343, 350 (2001–2002).

20. *Kaufman & Broad Communities, Inc.*, 133 Cal. App. 4th at 31–39 (identifying documents that are and are not considered "cognizable legislative history" in California's Third District Court of Appeal).

21. *People v. Garcia*, 28 Cal. 4th 1166, 1175 n. 5 (2002).

V. Initiative and Referendum in California[22]

Legislation in California can also come directly from the people through the initiative and referendum processes, discussed in Chapter 5 on the California Constitution. There are four required steps for members of the public to put an initiative on the ballot. The first step is writing the initiative, which proponents can do themselves. They can also get help from the Legislative Counsel's office. The second step is to get a title and a summary of the chief purpose of the initiative from the attorney general. If the attorney general determines that the proposed legislation would have a fiscal impact, the Department of Finance and the Joint Legislative Budget Committee must together prepare an analysis of that impact.

The third step is the one that most California residents are familiar with: circulation of the initiative petition to collect voter signatures. The number of signatures for a statutory initiative must equal at least 5% of the total votes cast for governor in the most recent gubernatorial election. Signatures for a constitutional initiative must equal at least 8% of the total votes cast for governor in the last gubernatorial election. The final step is filing the signatures with the appropriate county elections official, who must then verify the signatures to assure that they represent the registered voters in that county. Once certified, the measure is sent to the California Legislature. Each house assigns the measure to the appropriate committees, which hold joint public hearings. However, the legislature cannot amend the initiative or prevent it from appearing on the ballot.

Voters may also approve or reject legislation adopted by the California Legislature through the referendum process. Although the system is similar to that used for initiatives, there is an important timing difference. Referenda petitions must be circulated and filed within

---

22. This description of the initiative and referendum process is taken largely from the "Statewide Initiative Guide" found on the website of the California Secretary of State at http://www.sos.ca.gov/elections/ballot-measures/pdf/initiative-guide.pdf.

ninety days of enactment of the bill that is being referred. Initiatives are qualified by collecting the required number of signatures at least 131 days before the election.

You can track initiatives and referenda as they progress from initial proposal to certification on the California Secretary of State's website at www.sos.ca.gov. Click on "Ballot Measures" and then on "Initiative and Referendum Qualification Status."

For statutes enacted by initiative, when the text of the statute is unclear, courts consider the intent of the voters in interpreting the meaning of the statute. As explained in Chapter 5, courts look for evidence of the voters' intent in the ballot summary and the arguments and analysis presented to the voters in the California *Voter Information Guide*. Chapter 5 explains where to find these materials.

VI. Federal Legislative Research

Researching the federal legislative process involves roughly the same steps as researching California's laws, though some of the terminology is different. The United States Congress meets for two-year sessions, beginning on January 3 following a national election in November. Each session is divided into two terms, one for each year.

Bills are numbered sequentially in each chamber of Congress. Generally, Senate bill numbers are preceded by an "S," and House bill numbers are preceded by "H.R." for "House of Representatives." When a federal statute is enacted, it is printed as a *slip law* and assigned a *public law number*. This number is in the form Pub. L. No. 107–110, where the numerals before the hyphen represent the two-year Congressional session in which the statute was enacted and the numerals after the hyphen are assigned chronologically. The public law number given above is for the No Child Left Behind Act, which was passed in 2002 during the 107th Congress.

The new statute is later published as a *session law* in a series called *United States Statutes at Large*, which is the federal counterpart of *Statutes and Amendments to the Codes* in California. Session laws are designated by volume and page number in *Statutes at Large*, e.g., 115 Stat. 1425. Finally, the statute is assigned a *statute number* when it is codified with statutes having similar topics in the *United States Code*. The citation for the first section of the No Child Left Behind Act is 20 U.S.C. §6301.

A. Federal Bill Tracking

More Congressional material is available daily via the Internet, and using Internet sources for bill tracking is often easier than using print sources. The Library of Congress site at http://thomas.loc.gov provides bill summaries and status, committee reports, and the *Congressional Record* (which records debate in the House and Senate). The Government Printing Office site at www.gpo.gov/fdsys contains bills, selected hearings and reports, and the *Congressional Record*. Coverage varies even within a single site, so check carefully.

B. Federal Legislative History

As with California legislative history, federal legislative history research begins with the statute number. If you do not know the statute number, use an annotated code to find it (as described in Chapter 6). With a statute number, you can find the session law citation and public law number following the text of the statute, which will lead to the legislative history of the bill as it worked its way through Congress.

1. Sources of Federal Legislative History

In conducting federal legislative history research, you are looking for sources that are often very different from the sources available for California legislative history research. Federal legislative history is found in committee reports, materials from committee hearings, and transcripts of floor debates, none of which exist in California. Congressional committee reports are often lengthy documents that contain the committee's analysis of the bill, the reasons for enacting it, and the views of any members who disagreed with those reasons. Congressional hearing materials include transcripts from the proceedings as well as documents such as prepared testimony and exhibits. These documents may be available in local federal depository libraries, but not all libraries are likely to have all reports and hearing materials.

Unlike the *Journal of the Senate* and the *Journal of the Assembly* in California, which print only records of votes without any transcripts of debates, the *Congressional Record* publishes transcripts of floor debates in the Senate and House of Representatives. Be wary of relying on these debates, however, as it is impossible to know which legislators were present during the debate to hear the remarks. In addition, members of Congress may not actually have delivered their remarks in person; members can amend their remarks and even submit written statements that are published in transcript form as if they were spoken.

2. Compiled Legislative History

Researchers have compiled legislative histories for certain federal statutes that researchers or lawyers consider important. Two reference books that identify legislative histories of major federal statutes are *Sources of Compiled Legislative Histories*[23] and *Federal Legislative Histories*.[24]

3. Print Sources for Federal Legislative History

Table 7-3 contains the most common print sources for researching federal legislative history. Some of them contain a "How to Use" section at the beginning; otherwise, consult a reference librarian.

---

23. Nancy P. Johnson, *Sources of Compiled Legislative Histories: A Bibliography of Government Documents, Periodical Articles, and Books* (AALL 2000).

24. Bernard D. Reams, Jr., *Federal Legislative Histories: An Annotated Bibliography and Index to Officially Published Sources* (Greenwood Press 1994).

Table 7-3. Selected Sources for Federal Legislative History in Print

Source	Contents
United States Code Congressional and Administrative News (USCCAN)	Selected reprints and excerpts of committee reports; references to other reports and to the *Congressional Record*
Congressional Information Service (CIS)	Full text of bills, committee reports, and hearings on microfiche; print indexes and abstracts in bound volumes
Congressional Record	Debate from the floor of the House and Senate

4. Online Sources for Federal Legislative History

The sites noted earlier in this chapter for tracking federal legislation also provide useful information for legislative history research. The Library of Congress site at http://thomas.loc.gov provides bill summaries and status, committee reports, and the *Congressional Record*. The Government Printing Office site at www.gpo.gov/fdsys contains bills, selected hearings and reports, and the *Congressional Record*. A popular site for conducting federal legislative history is ProQuest Congressional.

Appendix 7-A. Final Bill History

This is the history of SB 255, which was enacted in 2001. The history is taken from the Office of Legislative Counsel website at www.leginfo.ca.gov/pub/01-02/bill/sen/sb_0251-0300/sb_255_bill _20011013_history.html.

COMPLETE BILL HISTORY
BILL NUMBER: S.B. No. 255
AUTHOR: Speier
TOPIC: Crimes: unattended children in vehicles.

TYPE OF BILL: Inactive
               Non-Urgency
               Non-Appropriations
               Majority Vote Required
               State-Mandated Local Program
               Fiscal
               Non-Tax Levy

BILL HISTORY
2001

Oct. 13	Chaptered by Secretary of State. Chapter 855, Statutes of 2001.
Oct. 12	Approved by Governor.
Sept. 19	Enrolled. To Governor at 3 p.m.
Sept. 12	Senate concurs in Assembly amendments. (Ayes 24. Noes 11. Page 2815.) To enrollment.
Sept. 5	In Senate. To unfinished business.
Sept. 5	Read third time. Passed. (Ayes 53. Noes 17. Page 3456.) To Senate.
Aug. 31	Read second time. To third reading.
Aug. 30	From committee: Do pass as amended. (Ayes 13. Noes 3.) Read second time. Amended. To second reading.
Aug. 22	From committee with author's amendments. Read second time. Amended. Re-referred to committee.

July 16	Read second time. Amended. Re-referred to Com. on APPR.
July 14	From committee: Do pass as amended, but first amend, and re-refer to Com. on APPR. (Ayes 13. Noes 2.)
July 2	From committee with author's amendments. Read second time. Amended. Re-referred to committee.
June 25	To Com. on TRANS.
June 6	In Assembly. Read first time. Held at Desk.
June 6	Read third time. Passed. (Ayes 26. Noes 10. Page 1468.) To Assembly.
June 5	Read third time. Amended. To third reading.
May 25	Read second time. Amended. To third reading.
May 24	From committee: Do pass as amended. (Ayes 8. Noes 3. Page 1217.)
May 22	Set for hearing May 24.
May 16	Hearing postponed by committee.
May 15	Set for hearing May 21.
May 14	Set, first hearing. Hearing canceled at the request of author.
May 7	Set for hearing May 14.
May 3	From committee with author's amendments. Read second time. Amended. Re-referred to committee.
Apr. 30	Read second time. Amended. Re-referred to Com. on APPR.
Apr. 26	From committee: Do pass as amended, but first amend, and re-refer to Com. on APPR. (Ayes 5. Noes 0. Page 657.)
Apr. 5	From committee with author's amendments. Read second time. Amended. Re-referred to committee.

Mar. 12	Set, first hearing. Hearing canceled at the request of author. Set for hearing April 17.
Mar. 5	Set for hearing April 3.
Mar. 1	To Com. on PUB. S.
Feb. 16	From print. May be acted upon on or after March 18.
Feb. 15	Introduced. Read first time. To Com. on RLS. for assignment. To print.

Appendix 7-B. Bill Analysis

The following excerpt is taken from seven pages of analysis produced by the Assembly Committee on Transportation as it considered SB 255. Lengthy omissions are indicated by asterisks. The full committee analysis is available at www.leginfo.ca.gov/pub/01-02/bill/sen/sb_0251-0300/sb_255_cfa_20010706_143350_asm_comm.html.

BILL ANALYSIS   SB 255

Page A

ASSEMBLY COMMITTEE ON TRANSPORTATION
John Dutra, Chair
SB 255 (Speier) - As Amended: July 2, 2001

SENATE VOTE: 26–10

SUBJECT: Crimes: unattended children in vehicles

SUMMARY: Makes it an infraction to leave a child under the age of six unattended in a motor vehicle, as specified, and creates a fund for an educational campaign regarding the dangers of leaving a child in a vehicle. Specifically, this bill:

1)Creates the "Unattended Child in Motor Vehicle Safety Act" and contains intent language stating that it is the purpose of this division of the Vehicle Code to help prevent injuries to, and the death of, young children from the effects of being left alone in a motor vehicle, to help educate parents and caretakers about the dangers of leaving children alone in a motor vehicle, and to authorize a monetary fine to be imposed on a person for leaving a young child alone in a motor vehicle in circumstances that pose a life safety risk.
***

2)Provides that the "Unattended Child in Motor Vehicle Safety Act" shall be known and cited as "Kaitlyn's Law."

EXISTING LAW makes it a crime for any person, under circumstances or conditions likely to produce great bodily harm or death, to willfully cause or permit any child to suffer, or inflict thereon, unjustifiable physical pain or mental suffering, or having the care or custody of any child, to willfully cause or permit the person or health of that child to be injured, or willfully cause or permit that child to be placed in a situation where his or her person or health is endangered. This crime is punishable by imprisonment in a county jail not exceeding one year, or in the state prison for two, four, or six years. Existing law also provides that no person shall leave standing a locked vehicle in which there is any person who cannot readily escape therefrom and that doing so constitutes an infraction.

FISCAL EFFECT: According to the Senate Appropriations Committee, the bill appears to redirect 60% of state penalties, county penalties and other penalties and assessments that otherwise would go according to statutory allocation for various purposes.

COMMENTS: This bill is premised on the belief that an educational campaign approach directed at social ills does not work unless it is coupled with an enforcement component.

***

Areas of Concern:

1)Most cases involving unattended children in vehicles occur on private property, such as parking lots and driveways. Law enforcement agencies might not have jurisdiction in such areas and, therefore, would be unable to cite for violation of this new law.

2)The first standard triggering the application of this new law (conditions that present a significant risk to the child's health and safety) is vague for lack of definition.

***

Analysis Prepared by: Joseph Furtado / TRANS. / (916) 319–2093

Chapter 8

Administrative Law

I. Administrative Law and Governmental Agencies

Administrative law is primary authority like constitutions, statutes, and cases. It differs from those primary authorities because it issues from the executive branch. Administrative law includes both regulations and adjudicatory decisions of governmental agencies. California defines state agencies to include "every state office, officer, department, division, bureau, board, and commission."[1] The online directory of state agencies lists over 500 state agencies, ranging from the Department of Alcoholic Beverage Control to the Workforce Investment Board.[2]

Agencies can be created in three fundamental ways. First, many agencies are created by the legislature. While agencies are generally part of the executive branch, the source of their authority is often an *enabling statute* passed by the legislature. Second, some California agencies are created, or their creation is authorized, by the state constitution. For example, the constitution created the Public Utilities Commission.[3] Such agencies are designated "constitutional agencies," and the usual rules of administrative law do not apply to them. Third, other agencies may be created by voter initiative. For example, in

---

1. Cal. Gov't Code Ann. § 11000 (Deering 2010).
2. The State Agencies Directory can be found at www.ca.gov/Apps/Agencies.aspx. Not all of the state agencies listed exercise all the functions discussed below. Although all of these bodies qualify as "state agencies," the California Code of Regulations (CCR) currently includes regulations from only 182 agencies.
3. *See* Cal. Const. art. XII.

1984 a voter initiative amended the California Constitution to authorize the California State Lottery and enacted the California State Lottery Act of 1984.[4] That act created the Lottery Commission, the agency that operates the lottery.[5]

The statutory and constitutional provisions that create agencies establish the powers and duties of the agencies. Each agency must work within the limits set by its enabling statute or provision; all actions taken and regulations issued by an agency that exceed the powers granted in the enabling law are void.[6]

Unlike other parts of the government, administrative agencies can perform all three governmental functions—legislative, executive, and judicial. Agencies exercise a legislative function when they promulgate regulations that interpret and apply statutes; these regulations are similar in form and have similar authority to statutes. In fact, California regulations are often referred to as "quasi-legislative rules." Agencies are part of the executive branch of the government, so they also exercise executive authority. Examples of this authority are licensing people to practice professions, such as architecture and cosmetology, and conducting investigations to see whether laws are being followed, such as anti-poaching operations by the Department of Fish and Game. Agencies also hold quasi-judicial hearings to apply the agency's rules in specific cases, such as the denial of government benefits. These hearings are similar to court proceedings, but are less formal.

In general, agencies function within the bounds of an Administrative Procedure Act (APA). California's APA can be found in the Government Code at sections 11340–11361. Some agencies and the actions of some agencies are exempt from the APA under section 11340.9 and sections 11351–11361, although many of these exemp-

---

4. *See* Cal. Const. art. IV, § 19, subd. (d); Cal. Gov't Code Ann. §§ 8880–8880.72 (Deering 2010 & Supp. 2013); *see also* California Ballot Pamphlet, 1984 General Election, at http://librarysource.uchastings.edu/ballot_pdf/1984g.pdf.

5. Cal. Gov't Code Ann. § 8880.15. Be sure to research the enabling statute or provision for all agencies, including those authorized by the California Constitution or a voter initiative.

6. *Morris v. Williams*, 67 Cal. 2d 733, 748 (1967).

tions have their own exceptions. These exemptions and exceptions apply, for example, to California's Public Utilities Commission, Division of Workers' Compensation, and Lottery Commission.

Each of the three branches of government has some oversight of agency actions. The legislative branch establishes agency powers and can add to them or remove them with subsequent legislation. The legislative branch also provides operating funds to agencies. The courts determine in contested cases whether agencies' operations and rules are authorized by their enabling acts. The governor supervises all state agencies, and the executive branch exercises control over many agencies by appointing their highest officials.

II. Administrative Regulations

The California APA establishes not only the procedures for adopting, amending, and appealing agency regulations, but also the Office of Administrative Law (OAL) in the executive branch. The functions of the OAL are to make sure that citizens can understand the regulations as written, that regulations are authorized by statute, and that they are consistent with other law. All proposed regulations must be approved by the OAL before they are filed with the Secretary of State's office, and the OAL can disapprove proposed regulations.[7]

All regulations are subject to the APA's rulemaking procedures. A regulation is "every rule, regulation, order, or standard of general application or amendment, supplement, or revision of any rule, regulation, order, or standard adopted by any state agency to implement, interpret, or make specific the law enforced or administered by it, or to govern its procedure."[8] Or, as the OAL itself says, "If a rule looks like a regulation, reads like a regulation, and acts like a regulation, it

---

7. Agencies can appeal these disapprovals to the governor. A link to the governor's resulting decisions can be found on the OAL website at www.oal.ca.gov.

8. Cal. Gov't Code Ann. § 11342.600 (Deering 2010).

will be treated by the courts as a regulation whether or not the issuing agency so labeled it."[9]

Agencies promulgate regulations to implement a statute, to interpret a statute, or to make a statute specific. Agencies are the "experts" in the field, so the legislature leaves to the agency the task of supplying the details that the legislature is not able to include in the more general statute. (See Table 8-1.) Regulations may also provide guidance based on an agency's understanding of a relevant statute or determine procedural deadlines and format for agency filings.

Table 8-1. Example of the Relationship between Statutes and Regulations

Statute: Because of the importance of agriculture to the California economy, the legislature enacted a law addressing "Certification, Processing and Canning, and Canned Foods." Under the terms of the statute, the Department of Food and Agriculture, an agency, was directed to establish standards for processing various agricultural products, including tomatoes.

Regulation: A regulation issued by the Department of Food and Agriculture specifies that "Any load of tomatoes which is offered for delivery to a canner shall be rejected and turned back to the grower if in excess of 2 percent, by weight, is affected by worm damage. A tomato is scoreable for worm damage when a worm has penetrated the flesh."

Sources: Cal. Food & Agric. Code Ann. §40761(a) (Deering 1997); Cal. Code Regs. tit. 3, §1332.1 (2013).

Once a regulation is promulgated, it is published in the California Code of Regulations (CCR), which is divided into titles. The titles are then subdivided in an outline format that may include divisions, chapters, subchapters, groups, subgroups, articles, and sections, al-

---

9. Office of Administrative Law, *What Is a Regulation?* 2 (Apr. 6, 2006) (available at www.oal.ca.gov/publications.htm) (citing *St. Water Resources Control Bd. v. Off. of Admin. L.*, 12 Cal. App. 4th 697, 702 (1st Dist. 1993)).

though a division may use only some of these subdivisions. Regardless of the outline format chosen, the sections within a particular title are numbered consecutively from one to the highest number. For example, the regulation discussed in Table 8-1 can be found in Title 3 at § 1332.1. (See Table 8-2 for a list of the CCR titles.)

Although regulations and statutes are both primary authority, regulations are subordinate to statutes. In any inconsistency between a regulation and a statute, the statute has priority.

Table 8-2. California Code of Regulations Titles

Titles

1. General Provisions	15. Crime Prevention and Corrections
2. Administration	
3. Food and Agriculture	16. Professional and Vocational
4. Business Regulations	17. Public Health
5. Education	18. Public Revenues
6. Governor [no regulations filed]	19. Public Safety
7. Harbors and Navigation	20. Public Utilities and Energy
8. Industrial Relations	21. Public Works
9. Rehabilitative and Developmental Service	22. Social Security
	23. Water
10. Investment	24. Building Standards*
11. Law	25. Housing and Community
12. Military and Veterans Affairs	26. Toxics
13. Motor Vehicles	27. Environmental Protection
14. Natural Resources	28. Managed Health Care

* Title 24 is now published by the California Building Standards Commission. The Commission republishes Title 24 in its entirety every three years. It is available in print, and some parts are available online at the Commission's website at www.bsc.ca.gov.

III. Researching California Administrative Regulations

The process for researching California administrative law is outlined in Table 8-3 and explained in detail on the next pages.

Table 8-3. Outline for California Administrative Law Research

---

1. Find the statutory or constitutional provision granting the agency power to act.
2. Research case law to determine whether the agency acted within that power.
3. Find the text of the relevant regulation in the California Code of Regulations (CCR).
4. Update the regulation in the *California Regulatory Notice Register* ("Z Register") to find any proposed changes.
5. Find agency and judicial decisions applying the regulation in similar circumstances.

A. Underground Regulations

Given the expansive definition of a regulation cited above, it may seem impossible for an agency to believe any action with general applicability would not qualify as a "regulation." However, California agencies have routinely created policies or procedures that they believe do not have to be promulgated as regulations using the procedures established in the APA. These agency actions are referred to as "underground regulations," and they cannot be enforced legally. If you think an agency has taken an action against your client based on what you believe to be an underground regulation, you can challenge the underground regulation by filing a petition with the OAL. If the OAL accepts your petition, it will issue an advisory opinion, referred to as a "determination." You can also ask a court to enjoin enforcement of an underground regulation.[10]

B. Researching the Enabling Act

Assuming you are dealing with a properly promulgated regulation, the initial question in analyzing the regulation is whether the agency

---

10. Section 11350(a) of the APA authorizes any interested person to bring an action for a declaratory judgment to test the validity of a regulation.

that adopted it acted within its power. If that is in doubt, your first step in researching a regulation is to find the statute or constitutional provision that gives the agency power to act. Although this step comes first analytically, as a practical matter, it may be more efficient to find the regulation first and look at the authority citation following the text of the regulation to identify the statute or constitutional provision that purports to give the agency the power to adopt the regulation. (See the discussion of the CCR in Section C below.)

Once you identify the statute or constitutional provision that purports to provide the agency power to act, the next step is to find cases that interpret those statutes or provisions. This research will help determine whether the agency acted within the limits of its power in adopting the regulation. Chapters 5 and 6 explain the process of researching the California statutory codes to find constitutional provisions and statutes as well as annotations to relevant cases. Chapters 3 and 4 explain how to find additional cases using reporters and digests. If the agency's power is clear, skip this inquiry and move directly to finding and analyzing the relevant regulations, as explained next.

C. California Code of Regulations

The OAL is charged with publishing all California regulations in the CCR. The OAL has licensed publication of both print and electronic versions of the CCR to West. The print version is *Barclays Official California Code of Regulations* ("*Barclays*"). *Barclays* is published in three-ring binders; some titles have only one binder, while others may cover as many as four. *Barclays* includes the full text of all promulgated regulations. It is updated weekly through the *California Code of Regulations Supplement* (the "*CCR Supplement*"), which consists of insert pages for the *Barclays* binders.[11]

---

11. Each issue of the *CCR Supplement* is identified by *Register* year and weekly issue number, i.e., *Register* 2007, No. 30. The "Filing Instructions" for each issue of the *CCR Supplement* should be located in the Title 1 binder; check the date of the most recent *CCR Supplement* in your library's *Barclays* to find out how recent your pages are.

Another print source of information is *Barclays Digest of New Regulations*, which is published along with the weekly *CCR Supplement*. The *Digest* includes all amendments to regulations that the OAL has approved and filed with the secretary of state in a one-week period. The *Digest* is a useful source to check to see if a regulation you are researching has been changed in the recent past.

Researching California regulations in print is relatively straightforward. *Barclays* includes a "Master Index," which is published in its own binder and is usually shelved at the end of the entire CCR series. The Master Index is divided into a subject index and a "Table of Statutes to Regulations." It is best to search in the subject index by topic rather than by agency name because entries for specific agencies lead primarily to regulations about the organization and procedures of that agency. Entries cite regulations by title and section number, with the title number first, followed by a colon, followed by the section number without a section symbol. The Master Index is issued on a semiannual basis.

The OAL website provides a link to the electronic version of the CCR at http://ccr.oal.ca.gov that offers a number of ways to search for regulations. (See Figure 8-1.) If you are looking for a specific section, you can type in the title and section number. Alternatively, you can use a standard word search, which will bring up a list of every regulation that contains those words. You can also click on a list of CCR titles and work your way through the table of contents for each title. Finally, you can click on the agency list, which will bring up the name and address of every agency with regulations in the CCR. Under the agency's name and address you will find a hyperlink to the location in the CCR of that agency's regulations, which may appear in more than one title.

Once you find a regulation in either source, read the text of the regulation carefully. Many techniques used for reading statutes apply equally well to reading administrative regulations. For example, you should always look for a separate rule that provides definitions, be aware of cross-references, read the text several times, and outline any complicated provisions. Figure 8-2 provides an example of a California regulation concerning fireworks.

Figure 8-1. California Office of Administrative Law Website

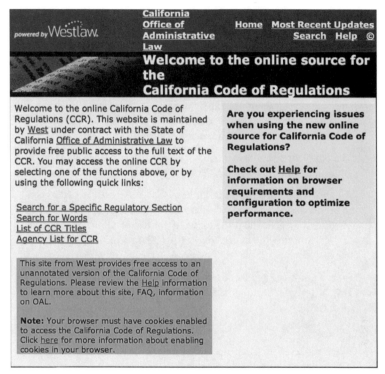

Source: http://ccr.oal.ca.gov/. Note that this website is maintained by West.

Following the text of each regulation is a "Note" that includes an authority citation to the statute that enables the agency to adopt regulations and a reference citation that indicates the statutes that this regulation implements, interprets, or makes specific. After these citations you will see a "History" section, which is provided whenever a regulation is adopted, amended, repealed, renumbered, or includes an editorial correction. Since the legal issue you are researching will be controlled by the regulation in effect when the issue arose, you need to read the history note to learn of any changes to the rule since that time.[12]

---

12. It may also be helpful to contact the agency that adopted the regulation and request the rulemaking file. The rulemaking file may reveal the

Figure 8-2. Example of a California Regulation

Title 19 Cal. Code Regs.
§ 986 Classification

(a) Fireworks or pyrotechnic devices that are to be used or sold for use in this state and found by the State Fire Marshal to come within the definition of "party poppers", "snap caps", "safe and sane", "agricultural and wildlife", "model rocket motors", "high power rocket motors", "emergency signaling device", or "exempt" fireworks shall be classified as such by the State Fire Marshal.

EXCEPTION: Special Effects items developed and compounded on location for single time usage.

(b) The classification of an item shall not be construed as conferring classification to any similar item without the approval of the State Fire Marshal. The trade name of an item shall not be changed without notifying the State Fire Marshal 30 days prior to such change.

NOTE: Authority cited: Sections 12552 and 12553, Health and Safety Code. Reference: Sections 12560–12569 and 12671, Health and Safety Code.

HISTORY

1. Renumbering of article heading, amendment of section text and new Note filed 4-14-92; operative 5-14-92 (Register 92, No. 21).

2. Amendment of subsection (a) filed 6-24-94; operative 6-24-94 (Register 94, No. 25).

Source: *Barclays Official California Code of Regulations*, volume 25, page 67 (2012).

---

legislative history of the regulation, including the legislative intent of the agency that adopted the regulation, any amendments to the proposed regulation as it moved through the APA process, and public comments on the proposed regulation as well as the agency's response to any comments received. As an alternative, a practicing attorney may rely on the commercial services discussed in Chapter 7 that compile legislative history for a fee.

D. California Regulatory Notice Register

Just as legislatures enact statutes throughout a year, agencies take regulatory actions daily. To inform the public of these actions, the OAL publishes the *California Regulatory Notice Register* weekly. It is commonly referred to as the "Z Register."

The Z Register serves several functions. First, it is the location where agencies are required by the APA to publish all proposed actions on regulations. These notices may include an "informative digest/policy overview" discussing the nature of the proposed regulation, a prediction of the likely cost to local agencies, a consideration of reasonable alternatives, and the effect on small business. The notices must include information on where the public can get the full text of the proposed regulation, when and where members of the public may submit comments, and the time and place of any public meeting. Second, the Z Register contains notices of general public interest, OAL determinations on alleged underground regulations, OAL decisions disapproving proposed regulatory changes, and a summary of regulations filed with the secretary of state.

The Z Register is available both in print and on the OAL website. Researching in the Z Register in print to find proposed regulatory action is difficult. There is no index or other finding tool for the Z Register. However, under the APA, agency action must be completed within one year of the date of the publication of the notice of proposed action. Therefore, a researcher needs to go through only twelve months of Z Registers following the first notice to be sure what happened to the proposed regulation. The issues for the year in which you are researching and for some of the preceding year may be available in your library. Z Registers from 2002 to the present are also available online on the OAL website in PDF format, and online research is somewhat easier. The OAL website provides a Notice Register Index that covers the preceding twelve months, for example. For Z Registers prior to 2002, you can contact the State Law Library in Sacramento.

The Government Code requires that all agencies that intend to undertake regulatory activity in a calendar year must prepare a rulemaking calendar by January 30 of that year. The combined calendar for all agencies becomes available several months later.[13] You can use this calendar to learn what administrative actions are scheduled for the upcoming year, which will tell you if you need to keep track of notices in the Z Register that might affect regulations that you are researching.

The most reliable source of information on pending regulatory action is the agency itself. You can contact agencies directly. In addition, agencies often have their own websites. Any agency that has a website is required by the APA to post information concerning its regulatory actions on the site.[14] If you need to keep track of pending regulations on a regular basis, members of the public and interested organizations can request a state agency to put them on a mailing list to be notified directly of any proposed regulatory actions.[15]

E. Agency Decisions

The APA not only controls administrative regulations and rulemaking, but also provides for agency adjudications.[16] Adjudications primarily involve decisions of those agencies that issue professional or occupational licenses and administer entitlement benefits; adjudications also concern personnel decisions of many agencies. Some adjudications occur through confidential mediation or arbitration. Other adjudications involve some kind of hearing process presided over by an administrative law judge (ALJ); these decisions become public record. California law authorizes both informal and formal hearings. Some larger agencies have their own ALJs, but others use a centralized pool of independent ALJs provided by the Office of Administrative Hearings.

---

13. The rulemaking calendar is available on the OAL website at www.oal.ca.gov. First click on "Publications" at the top of the screen, and then click on "Rulemaking Calendar."

14. Cal. Gov't Code Ann. §11340.85(c) (Deering 2010).

15. Cal. Gov't Code Ann. §11346.4(a)(1) (Deering 2010).

16. Cal. Gov't Code Ann. §§11370–11528 (Deering 2010 & Supp. 2013).

Agency decisions must be written, must be based on the record, and must include a statement of both the factual and the legal basis for the decision.[17] Since 1997, adjudicative decisions by agencies may be designated as precedential; barring such a designation, an agency may not rely on a previous decision as precedent.[18] Agencies must keep an index of "significant legal and policy determinations made in precedent decisions," and the index must be available to the public by subscription.[19]

Despite the requirements that adjudicatory decisions must be written and that agencies must keep an index of precedential decisions, finding such decisions is difficult. No method of printing, indexing, or digesting has been created. Some can be found on either Lexis or Westlaw. Agencies that have websites and issue decisions include precedential decisions and perhaps non-precedential decisions on their websites. But this means you have to know which agency's website to search and may have to look around the website carefully to find the decisions. Agencies will respond to direct requests, but you will generally need both a case name and a case number to get a useful answer.

Administrative orders may be appealed to a California Superior Court for review. California courts have jurisdiction to review the validity of both regulations and agency adjudications.[20] Conducting case research may reveal cases that address the agency rules and orders relevant to your research.

F. Attorney General Opinions

As the state's lawyer, the attorney general provides opinions that are similar to the advice of an attorney to a client. A formal opinion

---

17. Cal. Gov't Code Ann. §§ 11425.10(a)(6), 11425.50 (Deering 2010).
18. Cal. Gov't Code Ann. §§ 11425.10(a)(7), 11425.60(a) (Deering 2010).
19. Cal. Gov't Code Ann. § 11425.60(c) (Deering 2010).
20. Cal. Gov't Code Ann. § 11350 authorizes declaratory judgments as to the validity of regulations; Cal. Gov't Code Ann. § 11460 authorizes declaratory judgments as to the results of informal agency hearings; Cal. Gov't Code Ann. § 11523 authorizes review of the results of formal agency hearings through a writ of mandate.

from the attorney general responds to a specific question posed by a state or local public officer. The California Constitution and statutes restrict those who can ask for a formal opinion from the attorney general to constitutional officers, legislators, state agencies, state boards or commissions, district attorneys, county counsels, sheriffs, city prosecutors, and judges.

Even though attorney general opinions come from a branch of the government, they are not primary authority because they are considered advisory only. Courts may, however, find them persuasive if there is no relevant primary authority, and in that instance they are "entitled to great weight."[21] An opinion of the attorney general that has stood for a significant period of time may be highly persuasive because courts assume that the legislature was aware of the opinion and could have changed or clarified the law had it disagreed.[22]

Opinions are numbered as they are assigned to be drafted, with a five- or six-digit number that indicates the year and month assigned, and the order in which the opinion was assigned. For example, the opinion responding to the question, "may a city install and utilize an automated photographic traffic enforcement system in order to enforce a right-turn prohibition at an intersection" was assigned the number 11-1104, indicating that it was assigned in 2011 and was the fourth opinion assigned in November.

California attorney general opinions have been published since 1943 in *Opinions of the Attorney General of California*. There is a volume for each year. Each volume contains the text of opinions published in that year, a numerical table of opinions, a table of opinions cited, a table of statutes, and a subject index. Separate indexes were published for the period 1943–1972 and 1973–1982. Since 1983, each volume of *Opinions of the Attorney General of California* includes a cumulative index, with a ten-year cumulative index included at appropriate intervals. For example, the volume for 2002 includes the ten-year index and tables for 1993–2002. Similarly, the indexes and

---

21. *Phyle v. Duffy*, 334 U.S. 431, 441 (1948).

22. *Napa Valley Educators' Ass'n v. Napa Valley Unified Sch. Dist.*, 194 Cal. App. 3d 243, 251 (1st Dist. 1987).

tables in the most recently published volume for 2011 include references to opinions from 2002 through 2011, and the 2012 volume should include a ten-year cumulative index for 2003–2012. Attorney general opinions published since 1986 can be researched online at www.oag.ca.gov/opinions. You can perform a search using words, phrases, or the number of a specific opinion. You can also look through the yearly index from 1997 forward, which includes a short summary of each opinion. Finally, there is a Monthly Opinion Report on the site that lists pending assignments and provides links to newly issued opinions.

IV. Federal Administrative Law

The federal government's agencies function much like California's. Agencies such as the Securities and Exchange Commission, the National Labor Relations Board, and the Bureau of Reclamation administer the laws enacted by Congress, promulgate regulations that act like statutes, and adjudicate disputes in judicial proceedings.

The federal APA is codified at 5 U.S.C. § 551 et seq. Its goal is to promote uniformity, public participation, and public confidence in the fairness of the procedures used by agencies of the federal government.

A. Code of Federal Regulations

As in California, federal administrative rules are called regulations. Federal regulations are published in the *Code of Federal Regulations* (C.F.R.), which is published by the Government Printing Office (GPO). C.F.R. is a codification of regulations issued by all federal agencies. C.F.R. is organized into fifty titles according to agency and subject. Note that the subjects of C.F.R. titles do not all correspond to the subjects of the titles of the United States Code. For example, Title 29 in both U.S.C. and C.F.R. pertains to labor law, but Title 16 of U.S.C. pertains to Conservation, while Title 16 of C.F.R. addresses Commercial Practices. (See Figure 8-3 for an example of a federal regulation concerning fireworks.)

Figure 8-3. Example of a Federal Regulation

16 C.F.R. § 1507.3 Fuses

TITLE 16 - COMMERCIAL PRACTICES

CHAPTER II - CONSUMER PRODUCT SAFETY COMMISSION

PART 1507 - FIREWORKS DEVICES

Sec. 1507.3 Fuses

(a) Fireworks devices that require a fuse shall:

(1) Utilize only a fuse that has been treated or coated in such manner as to reduce the possibility of side ignition. Devices such as ground spinners that require a restricted orifice for proper thrust and contain less than 6 grams of pyrotechnic composition are exempted from § 1507.3(a)(1).

(2) Utilize only a fuse which will burn at least 3 seconds but not more than 9 seconds before ignition of the device.

(b) The fuse shall be securely attached so that it will support either the weight of the fireworks plus 8 ounces of dead weight or double the weight of the device, whether [sic] is less, without separation from the fireworks device.

Source: *Code of Federal Regulations*, Title 16, Part 1000 to End, pages 539–40 (2008).

C.F.R. volumes are updated annually,[23] with about one-fourth of them updated each quarter. C.F.R. is a softbound series whose spines and part of the cover are in color. Each year, the GPO changes the color of the volumes as it prints the new volumes. As discussed below, because C.F.R. is updated weekly or even daily in various online sources, it is often easier and more efficient to research C.F.R. online.

To research a topic in C.F.R., you may use the general index. Look up your research terms or the relevant agency's name, and then read the referenced regulations. An easier way to find relevant regulations may be to begin your research in either *United States Code Annotated*, either in print or on Westlaw Classic, or *United States Code Service*,

23. Title 3 of C.F.R. is not updated annually. Titled "The President," it includes executive orders issued during the year.

either in print or on Lexis.com. Both annotated codes include references to related regulations for each statutory section, if regulations exist. After finding a statute on point, review the annotations following the statutory language for cross-references to regulations. On Lexis Advance or WestlawNext, a search in the general query box will retrieve regulations as well as secondary sources, cases, statutes, and other materials.

The annual edition of C.F.R. is also available online through the GPO at www.gpo.gov/fdsys. The text there is no more current than the print versions, but the site allows searching by key word, citation, and title. You can also use the GPO site to access the "Electronic Code of Federal Regulations" (e-CFR). The e-CFR is an unofficial compilation of C.F.R. material and *Federal Register* amendments produced by the National Archives and Records Administration's Office of the Federal Register and the GPO. The e-CFR is updated daily. Finally, the subscription service HeinOnline (www.heinonline.org) also has a full C.F.R. database in PDF files; if your library subscribes to HeinOnline, you may be able to access C.F.R. through that site.

B. *Federal Register*

New regulations and proposed changes to existing regulations are published first in the *Federal Register*, the federal equivalent of the weekly *California Regulatory Notice Register* (the Z Register). The *Federal Register* publishes all notices of proposed rulemaking, including notices of proposed amendments to existing rules, notices of hearings, responses to public comments on proposed regulations, and helpful tables and indexes. Unlike California's Z Register, the *Federal Register* includes the full text of both proposed and final regulations. The *Federal Register* is the first print source to publish regulations in their final form when they are adopted (i.e., before they are codified in C.F.R.).

The *Federal Register* is published almost every weekday, with continuous pagination throughout the year. Each volume of the *Federal Register* covers a single calendar year, and page numbers reach the tens of thousands in the last few months of the year. The online version of the *Federal Register* covers the years 1994 to the present and is available through www.gpo.gov/fdsys. Both Lexis and Westlaw include the *Federal Register* dating back to 1936. The *Federal Register* can also be found through the subscription service HeinOnline, where coverage also begins in 1936.

C. Updating Federal Regulations

To update a federal regulation in print or on the government's website, begin with a small booklet or the database called *List of CFR Sections Affected* (LSA). As its name suggests, LSA lists all C.F.R. sections that have been affected by recent agency action. LSA provides page references to *Federal Register* issues where action affecting a section of C.F.R. is included. If the section you are researching is not listed in LSA, it has not been changed since C.F.R. was last revised. LSA is published monthly and is available online through www.gpo.gov/fdsys. First click on "Code of Federal Regulations" on the right hand side of the screen. Then click on "List of CFR Sections Affected" in the bottom left hand corner. From there you can view the monthly updates or you can search for C.F.R. sections affected by final or proposed rules that have been published in the *Federal Register* within the past twenty-four hours, week, or month.

Final updating in print requires reference to a table at the back of the *Federal Register* called "CFR Parts Affected During [the current month]." (Do not confuse this table with the "CFR Parts Affected in this [Current] Issue" located in the Contents at the beginning of each issue.) Refer to this table in each *Federal Register* for the last day of each month for all of the months between the most recent LSA issue and the current date. Also check the most recent issue of *Federal Register* for the present month. The table contains relatively general information (whether a "part" has been affected, not a "section"), but will note changes made since the most recent LSA.

Both Lexis and Westlaw provide versions of C.F.R. that are updated to within two weeks of the date on which you look at them. As discussed above, the e-CFR is updated daily.

D. Decisions of Federal Agencies

Like some California agencies, some federal agencies hold quasi-judicial hearings to decide cases that arise under the agencies' regulations or jurisdiction. Some of these decisions are published in reporters specific to each agency, for example, *Decisions and Orders of the National Labor Relations Board*. A comprehensive list of federal agency reporters is available through the website of Washburn University School of Law at www.washlaw.edu/doclaw/executive5m.html.

E. Judicial Opinions

The methods of case research explained in Chapters 3 and 4 will lead to opinions in which the judiciary reviewed decision of federal agencies. Additionally, C.F.R. can be updated to find relevant cases using Shepard's on Lexis or KeyCite on Westlaw. These citators are addressed in Chapter 9.

Chapter 9

Updating Legal Authority

Ensuring that the authorities found during legal research represent the *current* law is a critical step in the research process. A few examples demonstrate why: a case decided in 1990 may have subsequently been overruled, a case decided last year may have been reversed on appeal, and a recently enacted statute may have just been declared unconstitutional. These three authorities would still appear in online and print sources, but they should not be relied on in legal analysis. Determining whether an authority is current and respected is called *updating*; this step is sometimes referred to as "Shepardizing" because the first major updating tool was a print series called *Shepard's Citations*.

Updating an authority requires examining each legal source that has subsequently cited that authority and determining how the subsequent source treated your authority on a particular issue. A *citator* provides a list of citations to those sources that refer to your authority. Online citators provide the most comprehensive and up-to-date lists, so they are the focus of this chapter. (In fact, many academic libraries no longer subscribe to the print series.) Citators are also valuable tools for expanding research. By reading cases that have cited a relevant authority, you will quickly find other authorities on the same topic.

I. Online Citators

The two leading online providers of legal material both have extensive citator services. "Shepard's" is the online citator available on

Lexis; Westlaw provides a competing service called "KeyCite."[1] Their coverage of California material is not identical, though both cover cases, statutes, constitutional provisions, administrative regulations, and some secondary sources.[2]

A. Updating Fundamentals

The process of updating online is summarized in Table 9-1. Understanding that process requires familiarity with two basic terms: the *cited source* and the *citing sources*. The authority you are updating, in the following example a California case,[3] is called the *cited source*. The authorities listed in a citator that refer to that case are called *citing sources* or sometimes *citing references*. For each updating search there is only one cited source, while there may be many citing sources.

Most of the explanations in this chapter address specifically how to generate citator reports and how to understand them. In general, both KeyCite and Shepard's include color-coded symbols that provide a quick reference to researchers, indicating whether a particular authority is still "good law." While these symbols are helpful, they do not merit too much weight. A red symbol may mean that only a portion of the case was overruled; you can still rely on another portion of the case for a different point of law. Similarly, do not take too

---

1. Other online legal research providers also have citators: "BCite" on Bloomberg Law, "V.Cite" on VersusLaw, "How cited" on Google Scholar, "CASEcheck" on Casemaker, "Authority Check" on Fastcase, and "Global-Cite" on Loislaw. None rivals KeyCite or Shepard's, though they do offer less expensive alternatives.

2. The "Scope" link provides updated information about KeyCite coverage. The "Scope" link is located toward the bottom of the main KeyCite webpage. Shepard's provides a "Product Guide" that is available from the Shepard's tab by clicking the "Help" link.

3. While this chapter uses a case to illustrate the updating process, KeyCite and Shepard's cover statutes, constitutions, federal and California administrative regulations, law review articles, restatements, and many other legal authorities.

Table 9-1. Outline for Updating Online

1. Access the citator and generate a citator report (typically by clicking on a tab or symbol or by entering the citation of the cited source in a search box).

2. Select the type of citation list needed:

   • a short list for validating the cited source (to examine any negative treatment by later cases), or

   • an extensive list of all citing sources.

3. Evaluate the analytical symbols provided by the citator.

4. Limit the citator results by jurisdiction, headnote, date, or other function.

5. Prioritize and read the citing sources. Analyze the impact, if any, these sources have on the cited source.

much comfort when no red symbol appears, especially if your case has not been cited at all by later courts.

B. Reading Citing References

Be sure to read the citing references and decide for yourself whether your case is still "good law." While a citator can alert you to possible problems, only you can decide the impact of an authority on the case you want to use in your analysis. Thus, the most important aspect of updating is reading and analyzing the history cases and citing references.

With an online citator, accessing these references is easy. Click on an authority in the citator list to view the point in the corresponding document where your case is cited. Quickly skim that portion of the document and decide whether the source is relevant to your research. If it is, read the citing source carefully and analyze its impact on the cited case: Does the citing source change the rule of law in the cited case, perhaps by reversing or overruling it? Does it follow the cited case by simply restating the rule and applying it to a similar fact pattern? Does the new source distinguish or criticize the cited case? If so, why and how?

Sometimes a citing source does not address the legal question at issue in your research project. If a source analyzes only points of the cited case that are not relevant to your project, disregard that source. Reading and analyzing the citing sources provides research benefits beyond determining whether the cited case is still "good law." A citing source may have facts more similar to your client's situation. A court may make a point in a particularly helpful way. Or a citing source may raise a related claim that you had not previously considered. To take advantage of these benefits, and to avoid relying on quick-reference symbols to decide whether a case is still valid, include ample time in the research process for full updating.

C. Prioritizing and Narrowing Results

When time allows, you should read *every* citing source to determine its impact on the case you are updating and to see whether it adds to your analysis. When pressed for time, however, prioritize the citing sources you will read according to the following criteria:

- *Negative treatment.* Look for any case that reverses, overrules, criticizes, or distinguishes your case.

- *Jurisdiction.* Read cases from your jurisdiction before reading cases decided elsewhere, which are only persuasive authority.

- *Hierarchy.* Read cases from the highest appellate court, then the intermediate appellate courts, and finally the trial courts (if trial court cases are published) in your jurisdiction.

- *Date.* Start with more recent cases rather than older cases.

- *Headnotes.* Prioritize citing sources that refer to the headnotes from the cited case that are on point for your research.

KeyCite and Shepard's both provide filters that enable you to narrow the citing sources to those most important to your project.

D. Setting Alerts

Both KeyCite and Shepard's allow you to set "Alert" functions to notify you of action on an authority that you have updated. When viewing a document in WestlawNext or Lexis Advance, click on the bell icon to set an alert. You can customize the information you want to hear (e.g., negative action on a particular headnote) and determine how often you want to receive notice (e.g., daily, weekly), during what period (e.g., the next month), and through what method (e.g., online, email).

II. Updating Cases

The text over the next few pages explains the details of how to update cases using KeyCite, first on Westlaw Classic and then on WestlawNext, and using Shepard's, first on Lexis Advance and then on Lexis.com.

A. KeyCite on Westlaw Classic

1. Access the Citator

KeyCite can be accessed on Westlaw Classic in three different ways:

- through a KeyCite link at the top of the search screen,
- by typing a citation into the KeyCite box in the left frame, and
- from any source that displays a KeyCite symbol (by clicking on that symbol).

This chapter begins with the KeyCite link because it provides essential information, including an overview of analysis symbols used, a list of publications that can be updated using KeyCite, and tips on a number of KeyCite topics.

The KeyCite link connects to a page that is divided into left and right frames. The right frame explains the symbols used to show links between the citing references and the case being updated. Table 9-2 summarizes some of the symbols used for cases in KeyCite on both Westlaw Classic and WestlawNext.

In the left frame is a box for typing in the citation. To learn the citation format used by KeyCite, or whether a particular publication is included in KeyCite, click on the "Publications List" link in the left frame.

2. Select the Type of Citing List

The default citation list for KeyCite is called "Full History," indicated by an arrow next to "Full History" in the left frame. (See Figure 9-1.)

Table 9-2. Selected Symbols for Updating Cases with KeyCite

Westlaw Classic KeyCite Symbol	Meaning	WestlawNext KeyCite Symbol
Red flag	Negative treatment; the case is no longer good law for at least one point, e.g., at least a portion of the case has been reversed or overruled	Red flag
Yellow flag	Some negative treatment, but the case has not been reversed or overruled	Yellow flag
Blue "H"	Direct history for the case is available, and it is not known to be negative (note that these cases may have citing references, although that is not clear from KeyCite's current explanations)	
Green "C"	No direct history for the case is available; the case has citing references and they are not known to be negative	
Green stars	Depth of treatment (how much space the citing reference devotes to your case)	Green bars
Purple quotation marks	The citing reference quotes your case	Green quotation marks

Figure 9-1. Full History on Westlaw's KeyCite

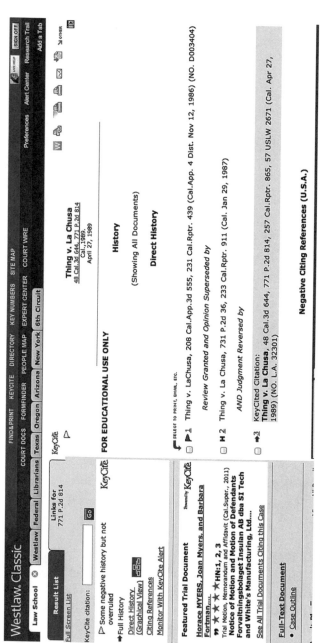

Source: Reprinted with permission of Thomson Reuters.

Despite its name, this list contains only the direct history and negative treatment of the cited source, not a full list of citing references. The first sources listed under Full History show the litigation process of the cited case, i.e., the direct history of the case.[4] This list of sources shows, for example, whether the case was affirmed on appeal or whether it reversed and remanded a lower court decision. Next in Full History, KeyCite lists "Negative Citing References." These are sources that KeyCite has identified as providing important negative treatment of your case.

With limited time to update a case, at least skim the sources appearing under Full History. To pull up a separate window showing the actual text of a source listed, click on the number immediately preceding that source's entry in the citation list. Similarly, to pull up the KeyCite page of a citing source, click on the treatment symbol (e.g., a red flag or a green "C") preceding that source's entry in the list.

The more comprehensive list of citing sources is called "Citing References," as shown in Figure 9-2. It is accessed by clicking on "Citing References" in the left frame. The Citing References page first lists those sources that have treated the cited case negatively, then those that provide positive treatment. Within each category, sources are organized according to green "Depth of Treatment" stars. Four stars indicate a citing reference provides an extensive discussion of the cited source. As the length of the discussion of the cited source decreases, the number of stars is reduced. Three stars indicate a less-extensive discussion of the cited source, while two stars indicate little discussion. One star means that the cited source is merely mentioned by the citing reference, perhaps in a string cite. Within star categories, citing references are organized by jurisdiction, court, and date of decision. A source that quotes the cited source is noted with purple quotation marks.

3. Analyze the Citator Symbols

KeyCite has assigned a quick-reference symbol to each authority that can be updated. The symbol is given both in the left frame and at the top-left of the right frame. These symbols are only preliminary indicators of whether a case is still "good law"; you must read citing sources that seem to bear on your issue and determine for yourself the continued validity of the cited source.

---

4. "Direct History (Graphical View)" provides that information in flow-chart format.

Figure 9-2. Citing References on Westlaw's KeyCite

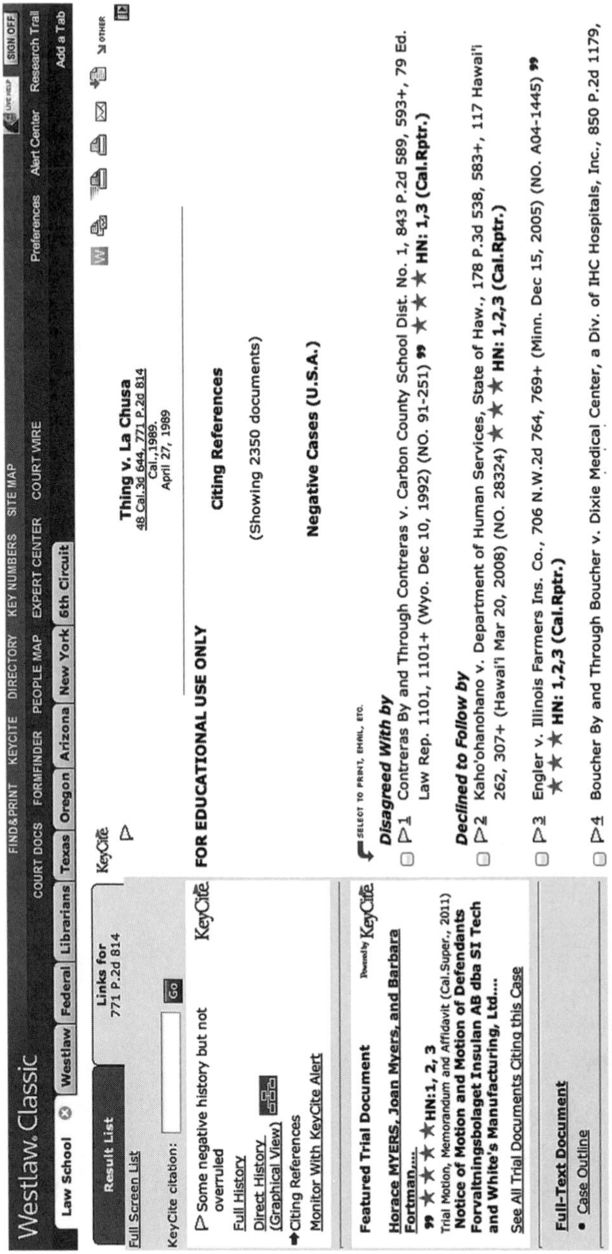

Source: Reprinted with permission of Thomson Reuters.

The same symbols also precede each citing source. The symbols located here show the KeyCite assessment of the strength of each citing source, as opposed to that of the cited case. If a citing source has a negative symbol, its impact on the cited case may be minimal; since other sources disagree with that source, its overall authoritative value is decreased.

Note that Westlaw includes in its list of citing references all cases that have cited to your case, even court of appeal cases without precedential value because they were never published or have been ordered depublished. You can spot unpublished cases because they will have a red flag in front of them and will have only a "WL" citation without a Cal. App. citation. Cases that have been ordered depublished may or may not have a Cal. App. citation, but they will at least have a red flag.

4. Limit the Search Results

Some authorities have been cited by many sources, and reading all of them is often unrealistic. For example, the *Thing* case shown in Figure 9-2 has over 2,300 citing references. To concentrate on the citing sources that appear most relevant to your project, click on the "Limit KeyCite Display" button in the bottom-left of the right KeyCite frame. This will bring up a "KeyCite Limits" page. The categories of available restrictions are listed in the left frame of this page. The citator list for *Thing* can be restricted by headnotes, locate (e.g., keyword search), jurisdiction, date, document type (e.g., cases, secondary sources, court documents), and depth of treatment. Click on a category to see its restrictions in the right frame of the page. Specify all desired restrictions and then click the "Apply" button in the left frame to see the filtered search results.

B. KeyCite on WestlawNext

1. Access the Citator

WestlawNext automatically generates a KeyCite report for each case that you open. The top of the WestlawNext screen displaying a case has three tabs for the different citing lists: Negative Treatment, History, and Citing References. An alternative for accessing KeyCite is to type "KC" followed by the case citation in the main search box on WestlawNext's home page.

2. Select the Type of Citing List

While KeyCite on Westlaw Classic provides two citator lists, the service on WestlawNext provides three. Negative Treatment shows any negative impact from cases in the same litigation or any negative references from other cases (i.e., in different litigation). History includes all cases in the same litigation, whether they had a positive or negative impact on the case you are updating. The History cases are available in both list and graphical format. Citing References shows all cases not in the same litigation that have cited the case you are updating; thus, there is overlap with the cases in Negative Treatment.

3. Analyze the Citator Symbols

The citator symbols used for WestlawNext are summarized in Table 9-2, earlier in this chapter.

4. Limit the Search Results

WestlawNext provides many options for narrowing the Citing References produced by a citator report. (See Figure 9-3.) From a drop-down menu, you can choose to view results organized by date (most recent or oldest first) or by depth of treatment. In the left frame, you can view the results by document type by clicking on cases, secondary sources, court documents, etc. Moreover, you can filter the results by search term, jurisdiction, date, depth of treatment, headnote, treatment status, and whether the citing reference is a reported or an unreported case. A "+" symbol next to a filtering option opens more possibilities, for example listing all of the federal or state jurisdictions in which courts have cited your case. Regardless of which filters you apply, be sure to read the citing references that seem most applicable to your project and evaluate their impact on your case.

Figure 9-3. KeyCite on WestlawNext: Narrowing Citing References

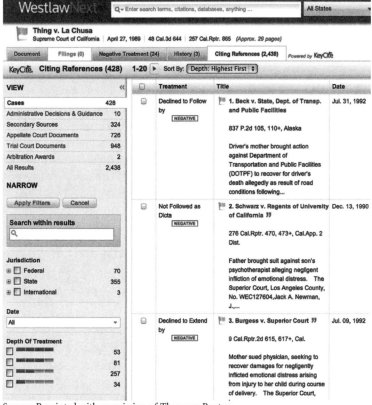

Source: Reprinted with permission of Thomson Reuters.

C. Shepard's on Lexis Advance

1. Access the Citator

You can access Shepard's on Lexis Advance in three ways:

- using the Shepard's link just below the main search box (to the right),

- by typing "shep:" and a citation into the main search box, and

- from any document with a Shepard's symbol or a "Shepardize" link (by clicking on that symbol or link).

Figure 9-4. Shepard's on Lexis Advance

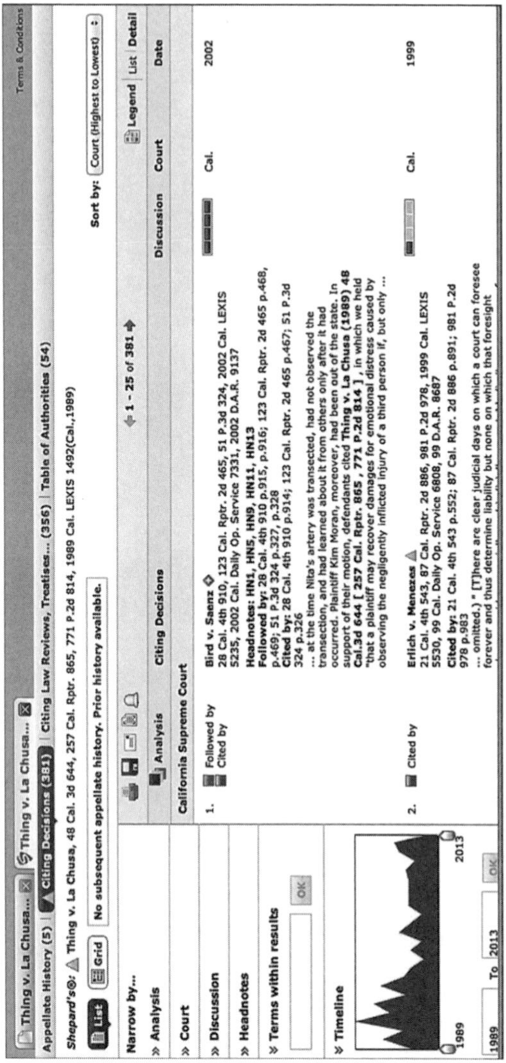

The Shepard's report appears with a tab marked with an "S" in a red shield (think of Superman).

2. Select the Type of Citing List

A typical Shepard's report for a judicial opinion will contain four lists, each with its own tab: Appellate History; Citing Decisions; Citing Law Reviews, Treatises, etc.; and Table of Authorities. (See Figure 9-4.) The tab for Appellate History refers to cases in the litigation involving your case; the material can be presented either as a list or as a map. The tab for Citing Decisions lists all other cases that have cited your case, while secondary sources and court briefs are listed under Citing Law Reviews, etc. The final tab, Table of Authorities, lists all of the cases cited by your case; while the list of Citing Decisions moves forward from your case to show subsequent decisions that cited it, the list in the Table of Authorities looks back to show the cases your case relied on.

3. Analyze the Citator Symbols

A "Legend" link at the top right of each list explains the colored analytical symbols used by Shepard's. In the Shepard's report, each symbol is accompanied by a word or phrase explaining its significance; the colors simply provide a quick visual overview.

- Red warns of negative treatment (e.g., your case has been reversed or overruled).

- Orange questions the continuing validity of the case, while yellow indicates some serious negative impact (e.g., your case has been criticized).

- Green shows positive treatment (e.g., the later case affirmed or followed your case).

- Blue suggests neutral treatment, which could mean your case was explained or that it was discussed in a concurring or dissenting opinion.

In addition to the symbols showing the type of analysis provided by the Citing Decisions, a set of bars show the "Depth of Discussion" of your case. Four bars means that your case was analyzed, three bars means it was discussed, two bars means it was mentioned, and one bar means that it was merely cited.

To the right of the name of each citing decision in the list, another colored symbol shows the subsequent treatment of that citing decision. (See Figure 9-4.) If a citing decision has itself been reversed, then it might not be as significant for your research. Lexis Advance does not include in its list of citing decisions court of appeal cases that were never published. If the supreme court granted or denied review and then ordered a case to be not published or depublished, however, that case may appear in the citing list.

4. Limit the Search Results

You can manipulate the data in the report to concentrate on the citing references that are most useful for your project. For example, using a drop-down menu at the far right of the list of Citing Decisions, you can organize the list by court, date, type of analysis (red to blue), and depth of discussion (analyzed to cited). As another example, you can use the "Grid" link at the top right of the Citing Decisions page to view the cases on colored grids. One grid arranges the cases by type of analysis and court, while another grid arranges them by analysis and date.

In the left margin, you can narrow the search results using a number of filters: analysis, court, depth of discussion, headnotes, search terms, and date (using the timeline filter).

D. Shepard's on Lexis.com

Shepard's is also available on Lexis.com, but because that platform is being phased out, the following introduction is very brief.

1. Access the Citator

Shepard's can be accessed from two points on Lexis.com.

- Click on the "Shepardize" link at the top of a document displayed on your screen.

- Click on the "Shepard's" tab from any screen and type the citation of the cited source into the box. For help with the format used by Shepard's, click on the "Citation Formats" link to the right of the box.

2. Select the Type of Citing List

Select the appropriate button for the desired list of citing sources. "Shepard's for Validation" provides a limited list of citing sources, intended only to show whether the case is still good law. To obtain a complete list of citing sources, click on "Shepard's for Research," which is analogous to KeyCite's list of "Citing References." At the top of the page of "Citing References," Shepard's provides a summary of how many citing sources were found and provides a breakdown of how those sources treated the cited source. By clicking on each category listed in the summary, you can view all of the authorities that treated the cited source in a particular way, such as "followed." When viewing the entire list of results from "Shepard's for Research," a case's "prior history" will be given first, followed by citing references arranged by hierarchy (highest courts first) and date (most recent cases first). Following case references, secondary citing sources such as law review articles are presented in alphabetical order.

3. Analyze the Citator Symbols

The top of the results page has a symbol that indicates the opinion of Shepard's attorney-editors regarding the validity of the cited source. To learn what a particular symbol means, rest your mouse pointer over the symbol. For a full list of symbols and their meanings, click on the "Legend" link in the bottom-left corner of the screen. Alternatively, scroll down to the abbreviated legend provided at the bottom of any Shepard's results screen.

Each Shepard's results screen on Lexis.com begins with a summary of results, typically in a grey box. This summary shows the number of times the cited source has been followed, distinguished, criticized, explained, etc. Clicking on one of these terms will allow you to skip through the search results to each citing source that treats your case in that way. To go to the cases that distinguish your authority, for example, click on "Distinguished" in the summary box.[5] The summary also includes the number of non-case citing sources, such as law re-

---

5. Some browsers do not support this function. An alternative is to use the "Find" function on your computer.

view articles, and the number of times each LexisNexis headnote in the case has been referenced.

Each citing source is shown with its own Shepard's symbol at the end of the source's citation in the Shepard's results list. Again, it is important not to confuse these symbols with the symbol for the case you are updating. The more useful symbol is the one at the top of the page that gives the Shepard's view of your case. Clicking a symbol next to a citing source will display the "Shepard's for Research" list for that source. Clicking on the name of the source will take you either to the first page of that source or the portions that refer to the cited source.

4. Limit the Search Results

Results can be sorted into lists of positive authority ("All Pos") and negative authority ("All Neg") using links at the top of the Shepard's page. You can filter the search results using "FOCUS—Restrict By," which is provided via a link at the top of any Shepard's page.

III. Updating Statutes

The basic process of updating statutes with KeyCite and Shepard's is the same as the process of updating cases: enter a citation on the appropriate screen (or click on the appropriate symbol while viewing the statute), review the sources listed, examine the analytical symbols (if any), restrict the search, and read the citing sources.

As with cases, both services provide more than one list. On KeyCite in Westlaw Classic, "History" provides legislative background, including reports of the legislature and the derivation of the statute. "Citing References" provides links to cases and other sources that have cited the statute. KeyCite in WestlawNext provides History, Citing References, and Context & Analysis. (See Figure 9-5.) On Lexis Advance, the three lists available for statutes are Legislative History, Citing Decisions, and Citing Law Reviews, Treatises, etc. On Lexis.com, Shepard's provides a short list under "Shepard's for Validation" and a more comprehensive list under "Shepard's for Research."

Figure 9-5. Statute Updating on KeyCite with WestlawNext

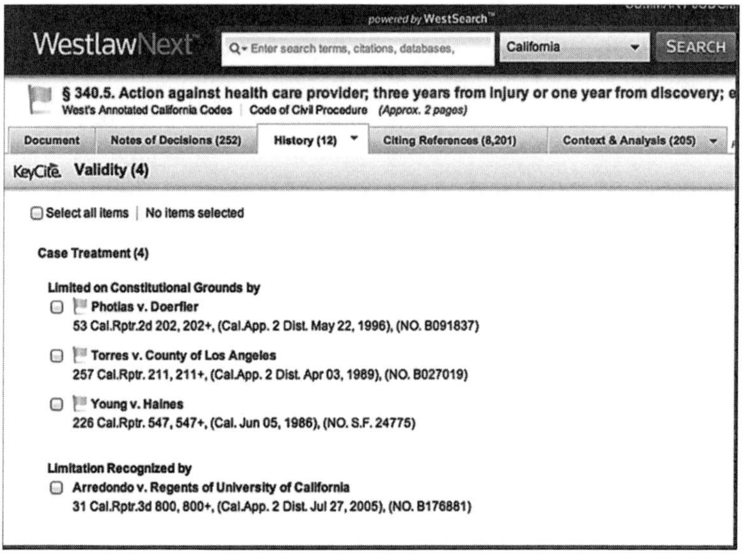

Source: Reprinted with permission of Thomson Reuters.

Both KeyCite and Shepard's provide colored symbols that suggest the validity of the statute; the precise meaning of each symbol is different from when the symbol refers to cases. For example, on KeyCite a red flag for a statute may mean that the statute has been amended, repealed, superseded, held unconstitutional, or preempted. Shepard's includes a unique symbol for statutes, an exclamation point noting negative case treatment.

When updating a statute online, begin with a citation to the smallest portion of the statute that is applicable to your research. For example, in updating the arson statute, California Penal Code § 451, you could update just section (a) instead of updating the entire statute; the more restrictive search currently produces about half as many results. If you want the legislative history of a statute, however, you may need to enter the code number without subdivisions (e.g., just 451). As with any updating work, the most important step is to read the citing sources to determine how they treat the statute that you are updating.

IV. Updating Other Authorities

Many authorities from other federal and state jurisdictions can be updated online, including statutes, regulations, administrative materials, patents, and secondary sources. Both KeyCite and Shepard's are expanding their coverage, so check frequently for current information.

Chapter 10

Secondary Sources and Practice Aids

I. Introduction

Sources are deemed "secondary" when they are written by law professors, practicing attorneys, legal editors, or law students; in contrast, "primary" authority is written by legislatures, courts, or administrative agencies. Despite the terminology, secondary sources are invaluable in legal research, especially in research concerning an unfamiliar area of law. Remember that the research process outlined in Chapter 1 includes research in secondary sources as the second step.

Lawyers use secondary sources to learn about the law and to find references to relevant primary authority. Beginning a new research project — even in a familiar area of law — with a secondary source may be the most effective approach for three reasons. First, a secondary source may provide an overview of the pertinent issues, aiding in the analysis of the legal problem. Second, a secondary source will likely explain terminology and concepts, making it possible to develop a more effective list of research terms. Finally, secondary sources often provide a shortcut to researching primary authority by including numerous references to cases, statutes, and regulations.

This chapter introduces the Witkin series, a source unique to California legal research; legal encyclopedias; practice guides, treatises, and other books; legal periodicals, including law reviews and bar journals; *American Law Reports*; continuing legal education (CLE) publications; legal forms; restatements; uniform laws and model codes; and jury instructions. The chapter concludes with a discussion of when and how to use secondary sources in legal research.

As an initial matter, some researchers find that beginning a new project in print secondary sources is more effective than beginning in an online database. This preference especially holds true when researching a complicated issue in an unfamiliar area of law. However, many of the secondary sources discussed in this chapter can be found on Lexis, Westlaw, and other online services. Some secondary sources are available for free on state websites. A list of helpful websites for California research is provided in Table 10-1. In addition, a quick search on Google or other search engines may produce valuable leads. A law firm may refer to key statutes on its website, or an attorney may have posted a helpful summary of a legal issue. Before relying on these sources, consider the questions raised at the end of this chapter.

Table 10-1. Selected Websites for California Research

Website	Address	Secondary Sources and Links
California State Bar	www.calbar.ca.gov	*California Bar Journal* CLE materials Bar forms Legal research links
Judicial Council Forms	www.courts.ca.gov/forms.htm	Mandatory and optional forms
Northern California Association of Law Libraries	www.nocall.org	Links to websites by legal topic
Witkin Legal Institute	www.witkin.com	Witkin products Current legal developments
The Recorder (formerly Cal Law)	www.law.com/jsp/ca	Legal news

II. Witkin's *Summary of California Law*

One of the most widely used and highly regarded secondary sources in California is B.E. Witkin's *Summary of California Law,* which is usually referred to simply as "Witkin."[1] While some researchers refer to it as a "treatise" and others think of it as an "encyclopedia," it is a unique resource that California lawyers refer to more frequently than either treatises or encyclopedias. Witkin concisely summarizes and examines California statutes and case law. Figure 10-1 contains an excerpt from Witkin.

Figure 10-1. Excerpt from Witkin on "Contracts"

[§179] **Binding Purchase Agreement.**

Whether an instrument creates an option or a contract of sale is determined not by its title or form, but by an analysis of the obligations imposed. (*Scarbery v. Bill Patch Land & Water Co.* (1960) 184 C.A.2d 87, 100, 7 C.R. 408; *Welk v. Fainbarg* (1967) 255 C.A.2d 269, 276, 63 C.R. 127 [held only an option].)

In *People v. Ocean Shore R. Co.* (1949) 90 C.A.2d 464, 203 P.2d 579, K (first party) made an agreement with M (second party), entitled "option," under which M was given "the exclusive right and option to purchase" certain property on stated installments, with the proviso that on default in an installment K could cancel and retain prior payments, but that K otherwise "shall have no right or claim against second party." *Held*, the agreement was merely an option and not a contract of sale. Despite the fact that M took possession and made regular payments, the language of the instrument showed a studious avoidance of any commitment by M to pay the purchase price, and he could not have been compelled to perform. (90 C.A.2d 469.) (For disapproval of *Ocean Shore* on the issue of whether an option is a compensable interest in condemnation, see 7 *Summary* (10th), *Constitutional Law*, §1138.)

Source: 1 Witkin, *Summary of California Law* 213 (10th ed., West 2005). Reprinted with permission of the B.E. Witkin Article Sixth Testamentary Trust.

---

1. The Witkin Legal Institute publishes other, more specialized surveys such as *California Criminal Law, California Evidence,* and *California Procedure.*

In print, Witkin is divided into sixteen volumes, some of which contain only one subject, and others of which contain a number of subjects. The subjects are not organized in alphabetical order; rather, the subjects appear in numbered volumes in the following order:

1. Contracts
2. Insurance; Workers Compensation
3. Agency and Employment
4. Sales; Negotiable Instruments; Secured Transactions in Personal Property; Security Transactions in Real Property
5. Torts
6. Torts
7. Constitutional Law
8. Constitutional Law
9. Taxation; Partnerships; Corporations
10. Parent and Child
11. Husband and Wife; Community Property
12. Real Property
13. Personal Property; Equity; Trusts
14. Wills and Probate

Volume 15 contains tables, and volume 16 is the index for all the volumes. To find an entry, review the softbound index volume using your research terms. The index will give you a volume number, a subject title, and a section number. Witkin is available on Westlaw and Lexis.

III. Legal Encyclopedias

Like other encyclopedias, legal encyclopedias provide general information on a wide variety of legal subjects. Legal encyclopedias are organized by subject matter under *topics*, which are presented alphabetically in bound volumes. Larger states tend to have their own encyclopedias; California's is *California Jurisprudence, Third Edition* (Cal. Jur. 3d). The two national legal encyclopedias are *Corpus Juris Secundum* (C.J.S.) and *American Jurisprudence, Second Edition* (Am. Jur. 2d).

To use a standard legal encyclopedia such as Cal. Jur. 3d in print, review the softbound index volumes for your research terms. The references will include both an abbreviated word or phrase—the topic—and a section number.[2] The encyclopedia's topic abbreviations are explained in tables in the front of the index volumes. Select the bound volume containing a relevant topic.

Next, skim the material at the beginning of that topic for an overview and general information. Then, turn to the particular section number given in the index and read the text there. Pocket parts sometimes provide updated commentary. Online, Cal. Jur. 3d is available on both Westlaw and Lexis.

The text of most encyclopedia entries is cursory because the writer's goal is to summarize the law. National encyclopedia entries will identify significant variations that exist between different jurisdictions, but they do not attempt to resolve differences or recommend improvements in the law.

In addition to describing the law, legal encyclopedias also provide citations to primary authority. California encyclopedias cite California primary authority. In Cal. Jur. 3d, cases and statutes appear in footnotes accompanying the text. Be sure to check the footnotes in encyclopedias for recent, primary authority. Because the footnotes in the national encyclopedias, C.J.S. and Am. Jur. 2d, cite to authorities from all American jurisdictions and tend to be dated, the chance of finding a reference to a recent, relevant case from your jurisdiction in either of them is limited.

An encyclopedia may also contain cross-references to other sources. For example, Cal. Jur. 3d and C.J.S. include cross-references to relevant topics and key numbers in West's digests. Similarly, Am. Jur. 2d cross-references *American Law Reports*, discussed later in this chapter.

---

2. Do not confuse these topics and section numbers with the West digest system of topics and key numbers discussed in Chapter 4.

IV. Practice Guides, Treatises, and Other Books

A book on a legal topic can provide an in-depth discussion of the topic and relevant references to primary authority. Legal texts include practice guides, treatises, hornbooks, and *Nutshells*. All of these books share the purpose of covering a particular legal subject, such as contracts or civil procedure. They are distinguished mainly by their level of coverage and their audience.

Practice guides typically cover an area of law thoroughly, but with a particular focus on the nuts and bolts of practice. Both treatises and hornbooks present a more theoretical approach than do practice guides. Treatises are generally more comprehensive statements on a subject than hornbooks, which offer a more summarized view. *Nutshells* are a series of books published by West that offer a very condensed explanation of law.

Thus, an attorney may use a practice guide or treatise to learn about an unfamiliar area of law. A law student may be more likely to turn to a hornbook or *Nutshell* to prepare for class or later to review concepts from a class lecture. This chapter focuses on practice guides and treatises because they are more commonly used than hornbooks and *Nutshells*.

A. California Practice Guides

California lawyers rely heavily on practice guides. Each one covers one area of California law in depth. The authors are typically judges or practitioners with extensive experience in the legal area they are writing about, and the text is practice-oriented. Table 10-2 provides a selected list of practice guide topics.

There are four major providers of practice-guides in California. The Rutter Group is the most highly regarded in many areas of law. Its guides are written by judges, justices, and lawyers. The Rutter Group also produces practice guides for areas of federal law. Figure 10-2 shows an excerpt from a Rutter Group practice guide. The other three providers of practice guides are Continuing Education of the

Table 10-2. Selected Practice Guide Topics

Selected CEB Practice Guides	Selected Rutter Group Practice Guides
California Domestic Partnerships	Alternative Dispute Resolution
California Estate Planning	Bankruptcy
California Juvenile Dependency Practice, 2012	Civil Procedure Before Trial
	Corporations
California Land Use Practice	Federal Civil Procedure Before Trial
California Tort Damages	Landlord-Tenant
Internet Law and Practice in California	Sentencing California Crimes
Organizing Corporations in California	
Wrongful Employment Termination Practice: Discrimination, Harassment & Retaliation	

Bar (CEB), a joint enterprise of the State Bar of California and the University of California, which is the largest publisher of practice guides in California; Bancroft-Whitney; and Matthew Bender. In addition to traditional practice guides, CEB publishes *Action Guides*, which provide lists of procedures for attorneys to follow in very specific situations such as "Handling Motions to Compel" or "Obtaining a Writ of Attachment." In addition to these providers, the California State Bar publishes some practice guides. For a list of the Bar's publications, visit the Bar's website at www.calbar.ca.gov.

National scope practice guides are published by the Practising Law Institute (PLI), the American Law Institute (ALI), and the American Bar Association (ABA).

Practice guides published in looseleaf binders are updated by replacing outdated pages. Some guides are published in hardbound volumes and updated with pocket parts. Still others are republished in full when they need to be updated. Always be sure that you are using the most current material available by checking the library catalog and browsing the shelves nearby. Almost all practice guides available in print are also available online through either Westlaw or Lexis. Rutter Group and Bancroft-Whitney guides are available only on Westlaw, while Matthew Bender guides are available only on Lexis.

Figure 10-2. Excerpt from Rutter Group Practice Guide: Civil Trials and Evidence*

---

c.   [8:460] **Effect of alteration of object:** Admissibility may be affected where the object has been altered in some way between the time of the incident in question and trial. In each case, the court must determine whether such alterations affect the object's authenticity. The court may decide that the probative value of the object is outweighed by risks of confusing or misleading the jury. [Ev.C. §352, *see detailed discussion in Ch. 8F*]

(1)   [8:461] **Adverse inference from destruction or concealment:** The reasons for the alteration are significant. Deliberate attempts to conceal or destroy evidence may result in adverse inferences against the responsible party: "(A) party's ... suppression of evidence by ... spoliation ... is receivable against him as an indication of his consciousness *that his case is a weak or unfounded one.*" [*Thor v. Boska* (1974) 38 CA3d 558, 567, 113 CR 296, 302 (emphasis added; internal quotes omitted); see *Cedars-Sinai Med. Ctr. v. Sup.Ct (Bowyer)* (1998) 18 C4th 1, 12, 74 CR2d 248, 254; see also CACI 204 (willful suppression of evidence instruction)]

[8:461.1] **PRACTICE POINTERS:** Instruct clients firmly and clearly in writing against destruction of any potential evidence relevant to ongoing or anticipated litigation.

Exercise caution when advising clients about removal of information from social media Web pages. Emphasize to the clients that they should print and save a screen shot of any relevant information and also copy the electronic version of the information to another server for preservation before deleting it.

(2)   [8:462] **Compare—innocent alterations:** Often, however, there are reasonable explanations for the alterations: For example, the object may have been damaged in the accident or altered in the course of testing by experts.

B. Treatises

Some treatises are so well known and widely respected that a colleague or supervisor may suggest that you begin research with a particular title. Examples of well-known treatises with a national scope include *Prosser & Keeton on the Law of Torts*, Wright & Miller's *Federal Practice and Procedure*, and *Moore's Federal Practice*.

Treatises in print are updated in a variety of ways. Bound volumes are updated with pocket parts. Treatises published in looseleaf binders are updated by replacing outdated pages throughout the binder with current material. Each page is dated to show when it was last published. Also, new pages at the beginning of the binders are often printed on different colored paper to draw the reader's attention.

C. Finding and Using Legal Books

Practice guides, treatises, hornbooks, and *Nutshells* can be located by searching the library catalog for the general subject matter of a research project. For a well-known treatise, include the name of the author as one of the search terms. When searching for practice-oriented material, use the name of the publisher (e.g., Continuing Education of the Bar or American Law Institute). Recognize that a number of legal books are available only in print format. After finding one book on point in the library, scan the other titles shelved around it for additional resources.

To use legal books for research, begin with either the table of contents or the index. In multi-volume treatises, the index is often in the last volume of the series. Locate your research terms and record the references given. A reference may be to a page number, section number, or paragraph number, depending on the publisher. The table of contents or index should indicate which type of number is referenced. Turn to that part of the book, read the text, and note any pertinent primary authority cited in the footnotes.

The authoritative value of a book depends largely on the reputation of the author. For example, one of the authors of the well-regarded, multi-volume treatise *Marsh's California Corporation Law* is a partner in the high-profile Silicon Valley law firm of Wilson, Sonsini, Goodrich & Rosati. In contrast, a *Nutshell* on corporations is designed as a study guide for students or a quick overview for practitioners; it is not considered authoritative.

V. Legal Periodicals

A. Law Reviews and Law Journals

Law reviews and law journals publish scholarly articles written by law professors, judges, practitioners, and students. Each article covers a specific legal issue in detail. Without the constraints of representing a client's interests or deciding a particular case, an author is able to explore whether the laws currently in force are the best legal rules and to propose changes.

Reading articles published in law reviews and journals can provide a thorough understanding of current law because the authors often explain the existing law before making their recommendations. These articles may also identify weaknesses or new trends in the law that might address your client's situation. The many footnotes in law review and law journal articles can provide excellent summaries of relevant research. Articles written by students are called "Notes" or "Comments." Although not as authoritative as articles written by recognized experts, student articles can provide clear and careful analysis, and their footnotes are valuable research tools.

Some shorter law review pieces, generally written by students, simply summarize a recent case that the publication's editors consider important. These are called "Case Notes" or "Recent Developments." They notify readers of important developments in the law but do not analyze or critique the case in any depth. They are often not helpful beyond offering a short summary of the case and the court's analysis.

Law reviews and law journals are generally published by law students who were selected according to grades or through a competition for membership on the editorial board. Many law reviews have general audiences and cover a broad range of topics; an example is the *McGeorge Law Review*. Many other law journals focus on a specific area of law; examples include the *Hastings Race and Poverty Law Journal*, the *Loyola of Los Angeles Entertainment Law Review*, and the *Berkeley Journal of International Law*. Still other law journals are "peer edited," meaning that law professors select and edit the articles to be published. Examples of this type of law journal are the *Journal of Legal Education* and *Legal Communication & Rhetoric: JALWD*.

Most periodicals are published first in softbound booklets. Later, several issues will be bound into a single volume. Articles are located by volume number, the name of the journal, and the first page of the article. Increasingly, law journals are moving to online publication only. Articles may be located on the law journals' websites as well as on Lexis, Westlaw, HeinOnline, and other online services.

Law review and law journal articles are not "updated" in the usual sense. You can, however, find out whether an article has been cited favorably or unfavorably by using a citator such as Shepard's on Lexis or KeyCite on Westlaw. Citators are covered in Chapter 9.

B. Bar Journals

Each state's bar journal contains articles of particular interest to attorneys practicing in that state. The California State Bar publishes the *California Bar Journal*. The American Bar Association publishes the *ABA Journal*, which has articles of general interest to attorneys across the nation. Articles in bar journals are often shorter than articles published in law reviews and do not have the extensive footnotes found in law review articles. Moreover, the bar journal articles have a practitioner's focus.

C. Locating Articles

Periodical indexes have traditionally offered the most accurate way of locating relevant articles. These indexes use specific subject headings into which various articles are classified.

Two of the more popular indexes of legal periodicals are the *Current Law Index* (CLI) and the *Index to Legal Periodicals and Books* (ILPB), previously called the *Index to Legal Periodicals*.

Full-text searching is available on Westlaw, Lexis, and other services, and the more sophisticated search engines can return accurate results. Techniques discussed in Chapter 2 of this text can be used to search for articles and to filter results.

HeinOnline offers full-text searching of a large number of journal articles, although it does not usually contain articles published within the preceding two years. The search engine is not as sophisticated as those available on Lexis or Westlaw, but it can be effective. One advantage to retrieving articles from HeinOnline is that the text is provided in PDF format, meaning that pagination looks exactly like the print copy (which makes citation of pinpoint pages easier) and footnotes accompany the relevant text (rather than being placed at the end of the article). Many law school libraries subscribe to HeinOnline, making it free to students and patrons. The website is www.heinonline.org.

Another site that is free to everyone is Google Scholar. It indexes a vast number of articles on a broad array of scholarly topics. To open an article, the researcher is usually linked to a site like HeinOnline, ERIC (the Education Resources Information Center), or SSRN (the Social Science Research Network, which includes articles that have not yet been published).

VI. *American Law Reports*

American Law Reports (A.L.R.) is a hybrid resource, offering both commentary on certain legal subjects and the full text of a published case on each subject.[3] Because cases are so readily available from other sources, most lawyers use A.L.R. almost exclusively for its commentary and research aids.

---

3. Each annotation is accompanied by a full-length case. This case may contain different editorial enhancements from those in a reporter, but the court's opinion will be exactly the same. While the annotation and case used to be published close together in A.L.R., reported cases now appear in a separate section at the end of each volume.

The commentary articles are called *annotations*. They tend to focus on very narrow topics, take a practitioner's view, and provide a survey of the law in different jurisdictions. Thus, an annotation on the exact topic of your research is likely to be extremely helpful. Annotations are written by lawyers who are knowledgeable, but who are not necessarily recognized experts. Figure 10-3 shows an excerpt from an annotation that explores one requirement for recovery under the tort "negligent infliction of emotional distress"—the immediacy of the bystander's perception of the accident. The annotation begins with an outline, research references, an index of topics covered, and a table of relevant cases from various jurisdictions, including a lengthy list of California cases.

A.L.R. has been published in several series over time. Early series contained both state and federal subjects. Currently, federal subjects are included in *A.L.R. Federal*, now in its second series. State subjects are discussed in numbered series: A.L.R.3d through A.L.R.6th. *A.L.R. International* began in 2010 and has published two volumes a year since then.

To locate an A.L.R. series in your library, search the library catalog for "American Law Reports." Often, the most effective tool for locating annotations using A.L.R. in print is a single-volume Quick Index for the series you wish to search. Alternatively, search the A.L.R Index, a multi-volume reference that covers the more recent numbered series and the federal series together. Another search tool is West's A.L.R. Digest, which includes references to annotations, practice aids, and A.L.R. cases. A.L.R. annotations are updated with pocket parts. Also check the Annotation History Table in the A.L.R. Index volumes to see whether an annotation has been supplemented or superseded by another annotation, rather than just updated in pocket parts.

A.L.R. and A.L.R. Federal can be found on both Westlaw and Lexis, although only Westlaw includes the first series. Annotations are updated regularly on both services by integrating new material into the existing annotation.

Figure 10-3. A.L.R. Annotation

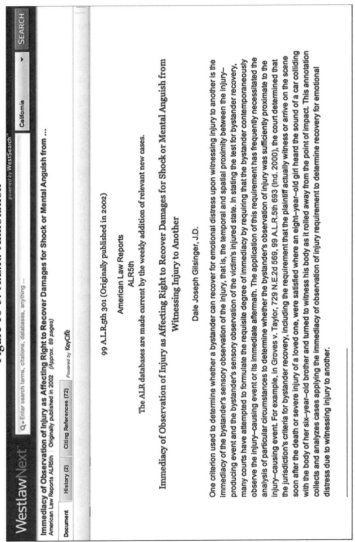

VII. Continuing Legal Education Publications

Attorneys in California are required to complete twenty-five hours of minimum continuing legal education (MCLE) courses every three years to maintain their membership in the State Bar. MCLE courses are led by presenters with significant practice or academic experience, and any course longer than one hour must include written materials; these could include sample forms, sample documents, and explanations of the law. While these materials may have very useful information, they are not readily available to those who did not take the course.

Some of the largest national publishers of similar continuing legal education (CLE) materials are the Practising Law Institute (PLI), the American Law Institute (ALI), and the American Bar Association (ABA). Locate CLE material by searching the library catalog by topic or by author, using the names of the more common CLE publishers as search terms.

VIII. Forms

Forms provide shortcuts in legal drafting. When you are drafting a document for the first time in an unfamiliar area of law, a form provides an excellent starting point by keeping you from having to reinvent the wheel. Forms are available from a diverse range of sources. Sometimes the best form is a document drafted by someone else in your law office on a similar topic. Both Lexis and Westlaw provide access to forms on many topics.

The website of the California judiciary contains links to a plethora of forms created and approved by the California Judicial Council. The forms cover matters ranging from domestic violence to probate. They are downloadable from the California courts' website at www.courts.ca.gov/forms. Forms are also available on some superior court websites. For example, the Los Angeles Superior Court's website at www.lasuperiorcourt.org has several links to forms.

California statutes provide forms for some particular situations. To find statutory forms, search the code index both for the substantive content of the form and under the term "forms." Legal forms may also be found in court rules, in practice guides (covered in Part IV of this chapter), and in CLE materials (discussed in Part VII of this chapter).

A "formbook" may provide actual forms or suggested language that can be used in crafting your document. Examples of California formbooks include *California Forms of Pleading and Practice* (Lexis-Nexis/Matthew Bender) and *California Civil Practice Guide: Civil Procedure Before Trial Forms* (The Rutter Group/Thomson West). Federal forms are available in numerous titles, including *West's Federal Forms* and *American Jurisprudence Legal Forms 2d*. Search the library catalog by subject for topical formbooks.

Take care in using any form, ensuring that it is current and in compliance with current law. Forms are designed for general audiences, not a particular client. Before using a form, be sure that you understand every word in the form and modify it to suit your client's needs. Do not simply fill in the blanks and assume that the form correctly represents your client's position. Unless a particular form is prescribed by statute or by a court, revise the wording to avoid unnecessary legalese.

IX. Restatements

A restatement is an organized and detailed summary of the common law in a specific legal area. While the *Restatement of Contracts* and the *Restatement of Torts* are the titles most familiar to general practitioners, other titles cover a broad range of topics. (See Table 10-3.)

Restatements result from collaborative efforts by committees of scholars, practitioners, and judges organized by the American Law Institute (ALI). These committees, led by a scholar called the *reporter*, draft text that explains the common law in rule format (i.e., they are written with outline headings similar to statutes, rather than in the narrative form of cases). The committees circulate the drafts for re-

Table 10-3. Restatement Topics

Agency
Conflict of Laws
Contracts
Employment Law
Foreign Relations Law of the United States
International Commercial Arbitration
Judgments
Law Governing Lawyers
Property
Property (Landlord & Tenant)
Property (Mortgages)
Property (Servitudes)
Property (Wills and Other Donative Transfers)
Restitution and Unjust Enrichment
Security
Suretyship and Guaranty
Torts
Torts: Apportionment of Liability
Torts: Liability for Economic Harm
Torts: Liability for Physical and Emotional Harm
Torts: Products Liability
Trusts
Unfair Competition

view and revision. The restatement that is published by ALI includes not only the text of the rules that embody the common law but also commentary, illustrations, and notes from the reporter.

A portion of a restatement becomes primary authority for a jurisdiction only if it is adopted by a court in a particular case. After a court has adopted a portion of a restatement, the committee's commentary and illustrations, as well as any notes provided by the reporter, may be valuable tools in interpreting the restatement. Cases in other jurisdictions that have adopted the restatement would be additional persuasive authority.

Lexis and Westlaw provide access to restatements. To find a relevant restatement in print, search the library catalog for the subject matter or search for "restatement." When working with print volumes, use the table of contents, index, or appendix to find pertinent sections of a restatement. The text of each restatement section is followed by commentary and sometimes illustrations of key points made in the text. Appendix volumes list citations to cases that have referred to the restatement.

A restatement's language is updated only when a later version is published. However, the appendix volumes are updated with pocket parts and supplements, and online restatement databases are kept current. Shepardizing or KeyCiting a restatement section will reveal cases and articles that cite the restatement.

X. Uniform Laws and Model Codes

Uniform laws and model codes are written by organizations that hope to harmonize the statutory laws of the fifty states. The most active of these organizations is the National Conference of Commissioners on Uniform State Laws (NCCUSL). Much of the work of writing uniform laws and model codes is done by experts who are law professors, judges, legislators, or attorneys.

Familiar examples of these secondary sources include the *Uniform Commercial Code* (UCC) and the *Model Penal Code* (MPC). Statutory language is drafted, then comments are solicited, and the language is finalized. The published uniform law or model code includes both the proposed statutory language and explanatory notes from the authors.

Generally, research into a uniform law or model code is relevant only after one of its provisions has been enacted by your jurisdiction's legislature. At that point, the provision becomes primary authority, and the explanatory notes become very persuasive secondary authority. That commentary could shed light on a statute in your jurisdiction that was based on the uniform or model language. For example, every state has adopted a version of the UCC. In researching California's commercial code, you could gain insights from commentary on the UCC that discussed the provisions adopted by California. Additionally, the cases of other states that also adopted the same UCC provisions would be highly persuasive in interpreting California's statute.

Uniform laws and model codes, along with official notes and explanations, are published by their authors. Additionally, commercial versions add commentary and often footnotes with case support. West publishes *Uniform Laws Annotated*, which offers indexing, text, and research annotations to uniform laws prepared under the direction of NCCUSL.

Finding a relevant uniform law or model code is similar to finding a restatement, and many are available on Lexis and Westlaw. In print, search the library catalog for the area of law, such as "commercial transactions" or "criminal law"; you may want to include in your search the words "uniform law" or "model code." In the stacks, scan the titles nearby to determine whether more helpful commercial editions have been published. Within the volume or set of volumes containing the uniform law or model code, look in the table of contents, index, and appendix to locate relevant sections. Often they provide section-by-section indexing of the uniform or model provisions, similar to a digest entry.

XI. Jury Instructions

At the close of a trial, the judge instructs the jury. These instructions outline the law; in other words, they tell lawyers what they have to prove in order to prevail. By examining the instructions in advance of trial, an attorney may better be able to present evidence to the jury. Even if a case ends before trial, knowing the instructions a jury would receive may produce more effective research.

Indeed, California jury instructions are often an effective starting point for research in an unfamiliar area of the law. In addition to outlining the law, each instruction is followed by annotations identifying the cases and statutes that support the instruction. The annotations also cite to relevant treatises and practice guides. These annotations provide a starting point for further legal research on the subject. See Figure 10-4 for an example of a California Civil Jury Instruction (abbreviated as CACI, which is pronounced "Casey").

Figure 10-4. Example Jury Instruction

Justia.com

Enter Search Terms   Search Justia

Justia > Trials & Litigation > California Civil Jury Instructions > Emotional Distress > 1621. Negligent Inflic Essential Factual Elements

NEW - Receive Justia's FREE Daily Newsletters of Opinion Summaries for the US S Courts & the 50 US State Supreme Courts and Weekly Practice Area Opinion Summaries N

California Civil Jury Instructions (CACI)

1621. Negligent Infliction of Emotional Distress—Bystander— Essential Factual Elements

[*Name of plaintiff*] claims that [he/she] suffered serious emotional distress as a result of perceiving [an injury to/the death of] [*name of injury victim*]. To establish this claim, [*name of plaintiff*] must prove all of the following:

1. That [*name of defendant*] negligently caused [injury to/the death of] [*name of injury victim*];

2. That [*name of plaintiff*] was present at the scene of the injury when it occurred and was aware that [*name of injury victim*] was being injured;

3. That [*name of plaintiff*] suffered serious emotional distress; and

4. That [*name of defendant*]'s conduct was a substantial factor in causing [*name of plaintiff*]'s serious emotional distress.

Emotional distress includes suffering, anguish, fright, horror, nervousness, grief, anxiety, worry, shock, humiliation, and shame. Serious emotional distress exists if an ordinary, reasonable person would be unable to cope with it.

New September 2003

Directions for Use

This instruction is for use in bystander cases, where a plaintiff seeks recovery for damages suffered as a percipient witness of injury to others. If the plaintiff is a direct victim of tortious conduct, use CACI No. 1620, *Negligent Infliction of Emotional Distress—Direct Victim—Essential Factual Elements*.

This instruction should be read in conjunction with either CACI No. 401, *Basic Standard of Care*, or CACI No. 418, *Presumption of Negligence per se.*

In element 2, the phrase "was being injured" is intended to reflect contemporaneous awareness of injury.

Whether the plaintiff had a sufficiently close relationship with the victim should be determined as an issue of law because it is integral to the determination of whether a duty was owed to the plaintiff.

Sources and Authority

- A bystander who witnesses the negligent infliction of death or injury of another may recover for resulting emotional trauma even though he or she did not fear imminent physical harm. (*Dillon v. Legg* (1968) 68 Cal.2d 728, 746—747 [69 Cal.Rptr. 72, 441 P.2d 912].)

Source: Justia website, at www.justia.com/trials-litigation/docs/caci/1600/1621.html.

California civil and criminal jury instructions are available on the California courts' website at www.courts.ca.gov; click on "Jury Service" and then click on "California Jury Instructions." Jury instructions are also available in print form from *California Forms of Jury Instruction* (LexisNexis/Matthew Bender) and they are available on both Lexis and Westlaw. Note that Westlaw continues to publish the predecessor rules, *Book of Approved Jury Instructions* or BAJI, even though the California courts' website makes clear that those instructions are no longer officially approved.

XII. Using Secondary Sources and Practice Aids in Research

As the discussions above suggest, use of the various secondary sources should be tailored to the needs of individual research projects. For a broad overview of an area of law, Witkin or an encyclopedia may be best. For in-depth analysis of a narrow topic, a law review article is more likely to be helpful. In litigation, court-approved forms and uniform jury instructions will be indispensable.

Consider your own background in the subject matter and the goals of your research, and select from these sources accordingly. How many secondary sources you use depends on the success of your early searches and the time available to you. Often checking one or two secondary sources is sufficient; you would almost never check every source discussed in this chapter for a single project.

Despite the value of secondary sources, they are rarely cited in memoranda or briefs. Some sources, such as indexes for periodicals, are not "authority" at all. Rather, they are authority-finding tools and should never be cited. Encyclopedias, A.L.R. annotations, and MCLE materials should be cited only as a last resort. Even sources that are authoritative, including Witkin, practice guides, law review articles, and treatises, should be cited only infrequently.

Secondary authorities are typically cited in just three instances. First, sometimes writers need to summarize the development of the law. If no case has provided a summary, citing a treatise or law review article that traces that development could be helpful to the reader. Next, secondary authority may provide additional support for a point already cited to primary authority. For example, you can bolster an argument supported by a case, especially if it is from another jurisdiction, by also citing an article or treatise by a respected expert on the topic. Finally, citation to secondary authority is appropriate when there is no law on point for an argument. When dealing with new areas of the law or when arguing to expand or change the law, your only support may come from a law review article or other secondary authority. Be careful in citing these sources. By citing secondary authorities, you are admitting to your audience that you could not find any primary authority supporting your arguments, which weakens those arguments substantially.

Whether or not you cite a secondary source in a document, you must decide the weight to give secondary authority in developing your own analysis. Consider the following criteria:

- *Who is the author?* The views of a respected scholar, an acknowledged expert, or a judge carry more weight than those of a student author or an anonymous editor.

- *When was the material published?* Especially for cutting-edge issues, a more recent article is likely to be more helpful. Even with more traditional issues, though, be sure that the material analyzes the current state of the law.

- *Where was the material published?* Respected publishers, whether found in print or online, almost always carry more weight than online websites by individuals or groups with a particular interest.

- *What depth is provided?* The more focused and thorough the analysis, the more useful the material will be.

- *How relevant is it to your argument?* If the author is arguing your exact point, the material will be more persuasive than if the author's arguments are only tangential to yours.

- *Has this secondary source been cited previously by courts?* If a court has found an article persuasive in the past, it is likely to find it persuasive again. The text of a secondary source may become primary authority if it is adopted by a court or legislature.

Remember that the goals of reading secondary sources are usually to obtain an overview of an area of law and to locate citations to primary authority. These goals can be met by referring to secondary sources in books in the library or by skimming them online, without the waste of printing out numerous pages of text. Moreover, some lengthy secondary sources—for example, law review articles—may initially seem helpful but after a few pages may concentrate on a narrow point that is not applicable to your situation. When working online, try to avoid printing a document until you are sure that you will need to refer to it repeatedly in your research and analysis.

Chapter 11

Planning a Research Strategy and Organizing Research Results

Every research project needs a defined strategy to ensure thorough and efficient research. This chapter quickly reviews the basic research process presented in Chapter 1 and then discusses how to modify it to design a strategy for particular projects. Next, the chapter moves to methods of organizing research results. An organized approach will keep you from getting lost in a sea of papers or online documents and will aid in your analysis of the legal issue.

I. Planning a Research Strategy

The research process presented in Chapter 1 contains six steps: (1) prepare to research; (2) learn about the issue by consulting secondary sources and practice aids; (3) search for primary authority—meaning constitutional provisions, statutes, administrative rules, and cases; (4) read the authorities carefully; (5) update your research by using citators; and (6) end research when all analytical points have support and when searches in different sources produce the same set of authorities.

The key to successful research is to not wander randomly through these steps; you might forget a step—and miss an important line of authorities—or you might waste valuable time. Instead, begin each project with a defined strategy that considers the legal clues you have as you begin, the sources available, and the goal of the project. These considerations are addressed below.

A. Asking Fundamental Questions

The first step in any research project is to prepare, which requires gathering the relevant facts, identifying the precise issue or issues you need to research, determining the relevant jurisdiction, and listing research terms. Be wary of skipping the step in which you develop research terms or trying to do it quickly in your head. If you know the cause of action—and the various ways that indexes or courts may refer to it—that quick approach may work. But some projects get off to a slow start because the researcher did not begin with a thorough list of research terms. If you do not find pertinent material in your early searches, you may need to go back to the beginning and develop a better list of terms.

When you develop your research strategy (essentially, a modified version of the general, six-step process) depends on the project. You might develop a research strategy before you undertake the initial preparatory steps in the previous paragraph, or you might need to do a bit of research first to know what strategy might be effective. In developing your research strategy, remember to ask the following questions, too:

- Is this issue controlled by state law, federal law, or both?
- Are there statutes or constitutional provisions on point, or is this area left to common law?
- Are administrative rules or decisions likely to be involved?
- Where in the research process will print sources be more efficient and cost-effective than online sources?
- What period of time needs to be researched?
- How long do I have to complete the project?

Answering these questions and writing out a strategy will likely make a new project feel less overwhelming because you will see discrete steps that you need to take.

B. Modifying the Process to Create a Focused Strategy

Chapter 1 pointed out a few simple ways that the research process can be modified to suit your research project. To expand on one of those ways, assume that a colleague gives you a citation to a case that is directly on point—a significant clue in your research. You should modify the basic research process to reflect what you know. You might write out a research strategy that looks like the following simple checklist:

- read the case
- read any statutes and cases it cites
- search with the key numbers on WestlawNext
- use KeyCite to update and to find more cases
- check for additional statutes (generate terms first)
- if statutes are on point, check for administrative law
- if any analytical holes are left, consider secondary sources

Your first step in this project should be reading the case, not generating research terms. Next, you may decide to read some of the key cases cited by that case. To find even more cases, you could use key numbers from relevant headnotes in the case to search in WestlawNext or using a West digest (in print or online). Then, running a KeyCite search could find even more cases and would determine whether the case is still respected authority. At some point in reading all of these cases, you may have come across a statute. If so, you should stop and read it, and review its annotations for more cases that may be relevant. You should also consider whether any administrative regulations have addressed the statute. If you have not yet encountered a statute in your search, you should spend a few minutes searching for one. At that point, you would need to generate research terms to search in an annotated code.

If you find strong support for all of your issues, you might never refer to a secondary source in this project. You may, however, decide to do a quick search of a state-specific treatise or practice guide, just to be sure you have not missed anything.

C. Selecting Sources

As you plan your strategy, decide which sources you will use. You should base this decision primarily on which sources are best suited for the task at hand, though you may also consider availability and personal preference. If, for example, your office has a contract with Lexis but not Westlaw, you will naturally choose Shepard's over KeyCite.

1. Researching an Unfamiliar Area of Law

When researching an unfamiliar area of law, you will probably be more successful beginning with secondary sources. Some common research questions and appropriate secondary sources for researching them are discussed next.

a. Typical Practice Issues

Lawyers are faced with fundamental practice tasks every day, such as filing a complaint, conducting depositions, drafting a will or trust, or making a presentation to a client about alternative courses of action. Two very useful tools in these areas are practice guides and state legal encyclopedias. Each is likely to give an overview of the area of law, practice pointers, and even relevant forms and checklists. In California, Witkin would be an obvious choice among available secondary sources.

b. Cutting-Edge Issues

Often lawyers have to address novel legal issues. (If the answers were easy and clear, a lawyer's knowledge and expertise would be less valued.) Sometimes the answers can be developed or derived from existing primary authorities, with the addition of some common sense and creativity.

If there is no primary authority on point—consider the first lawyer faced with the question of whether an email attachment satisfied a requirement for service of process by mail—a secondary source may be the only authority that has addressed the question in a meaningful way. For instance, the author of a recent law review article may have pondered the same question and produced thoughtful analysis of the issue.

c. Surveys

Surveys of the law in multiple jurisdictions can be powerful tools in convincing judges to modify existing law in a particular state. Surveys can also help persuade a court to adopt a new rule favorable to the client when no rule exists in your jurisdiction. A.L.R. annotations usually provide tables that list statutes and cases from every American jurisdiction that has considered a question.

2. Beginning with a Statutory Citation

If you know of a relevant statute, your research project is likely to be most effective if you go directly to an annotated code. In California, you will need to choose among the various online resources or between *West's* and *Deering's* in print. In practice, your choice may be made for you by what is available in your office.

3. Launching from "One Good Case"

Once you find a case that is on point, multiple sources are available for further research. If you are using print sources published by West, a digest will lead you to additional cases on the same point by using the topics and key numbers attached to each headnote. On Westlaw Classic, you can use the "Key Numbers" link to browse the digest online or to run a KeySearch through related topics.

Using WestlawNext, you can access the key number system by clicking on the words and phrases at the beginning of a headnote (the topic and key number) or you can click the link under the headnotes that gives the number of "Cases that cite this headnote." Another approach is to use the KeyCite tabs at the top of the screen for the case.

Similarly, on Lexis Advance, clicking on a hyperlinked phrase at the beginning of a headnote will produce a drop-down menu for topic searching. You can either "Get topic documents" (which can be narrowed with filters) or "View in topic index." Alternatively, you can highlight text and then choose from a drop-down menu to "Search using selected text." Finally, you can click on "Shepardize—Narrow by this Headnote" to jump into the Shepard's results for that case.

D. Choosing Between Print and Online Research

An important consideration is whether to use print or online sources. Some sources are frequently better in one medium or another, though you must also consider the resources available and your own proficiency in various search techniques.

Sources that are typically preferred in print are secondary sources and statutes. For example, a lawyer specializing in labor law will likely have a deskbook, practice guide, or some other quick reference book close at hand. Referring to that source in print will give the lawyer a head start in understanding the legal issues and thus aid in online research. Statutory research also lends itself to print sources. Many lawyers find that perusing the print index is more efficient than viewing the index online or constructing full-text searches.

As for researching judicial opinions, some lawyers still find print digests preferable to their online counterparts; however, the major fee-based providers (Lexis and Westlaw) have made such great strides in natural-language searching and topic searching that the print digests may not offer much analytical advantage. The key choice here will be based on costs, availability, and your personal preference.

Whether to read documents in print or online is an important decision. You might decide to skim secondary sources online, highlighting and saving them to folders provided by online services. You might do the same with cases as you initially encounter them. But many experienced attorneys read the leading authorities in print. You should try that approach if reading cases on an electronic screen does not lead you to a deep understanding of the law.

E. Sample Research Strategy

To put the discussion above in context, assume that you have been given as a new research task the problem posed in Chapter 1. Your client has suffered nightmares and anxiety attacks after the following scene at a restaurant in San Diego. He and his wife were having lunch at an outside table near the street in the Gaslamp Quarter. The man went inside to use the restroom, and as he was returning to the table he heard a car crash. He saw a table umbrella fall and felt pieces of glass from a shattered mirror. A car had jumped the curb and hit his wife. Although she eventually recovered from her serious injuries, he has continued to suffer symptoms. He wants to know whether he has a claim against the driver. Assume that you have not researched this issue before and do not know which cause of action might apply. A sample strategy is listed in Table 11-1. Of course, you could conduct a very similar search with primarily West products, selecting *West's* annotated statutes in Step 3, using KeySearch or a full-text search on Westlaw in Step 5, and updating with KeyCite in Step 6.

Table 11-1. Sample Research Strategy

- Generate terms. Don't know cause of action, but the general issue is whether the client can recover from the driver.
- Check Witkin in print; look for jury instructions online.
- Check for statutes in *Deering's* in print. Review annotations. If there are statutes, check for pertinent regulations.
- Skim cases referenced so far. Use Lexis Advance drop-down from relevant headnotes for additional cases on the same topics.
- Shepardize authorities on Lexis Advance.
- Create research chart to check analysis.

II. Organizing Research

Legal research often produces many documents that you must organize and analyze. Keeping research organized is a means to efficient research and thorough legal analysis. Organizational techniques vary among researchers, but the following discussion explains two methods that will help novices working on their first projects. While the first method focuses on print and the second on online, in most situations you will use a combination—writing out a list of sources you checked (e.g., books, various online services) but relying on each online service to keep track of specific searches, and using online folders to organize authorities as you encounter them but printing out the most important documents.

A. Keeping Notes and Documents in a Binder

Before beginning research, get a three-ring binder in which you will keep hard copies of the most important authorities you find in your research. Tab the binder with the following headings: strategy/process; list of primary authorities; secondary sources; statutes (include rules and constitutional provisions here); cases; updating; and outline. Consider using color-coded sticky notes to tab each new document so that you can find it easily.

As you begin research, create a process trail (this is similar to the "history" created online by Westlaw and Lexis). This document will record what you actually do as you work through the project. Start with your research strategy document and turn it into a quick summary of what you've done. Each time you move to a new step in your research strategy or work with a new resource, make notes in your process trail that summarize your work. For print research, include the volumes you used, the indexes or tables you reviewed, and the terms you searched for. For computer research, include the site, the specific database or link, and the searches that you entered. List both successful and unsuccessful index terms and searches so that (1) you do not inadvertently repeat these same steps later, and (2) you can revisit a seemingly tangential issue that later seems relevant. Table 11-2 develops a very brief process trail for the research strategy given in Table 11-1. (Yours should be more thorough.) Note that Table 1-3 in Chapter 1 contains a more thorough list of research terms.

Table 11-2. Process Trail

- Generate terms: anxiety from watching spouse injured; legal theory is likely under a form of negligence.
- Check Witkin in print. Use Table of Contents:

    Torts, Negligence: General Duty, Negligent Causing of Emotional Distress.

    Sections 1022-1023; found *Dillon, Wong, Wooden, Lawson.*

    Jury instructions: found CACI 1621 on Cal. courts website.
- Check for statutes in *Deering's* in print. No statutes on this topic.
- Skim cases referenced so far: *Dillon, Thing.*
- Shepardize on Lexis Advance. *Thing* led to *Bird* and *Air Crash.*
- Create a research chart to check analysis (see Table 11-3).

Create a list that contains the name and citation for each of the primary authorities that you need to read. Throughout your research, as you come across a potentially relevant authority, include it on the list. This method will allow you to maintain your train of thought with one resource while ensuring that you keep track of important authorities to check later. After creating a list that includes a number of sources, check for duplicates before reading the authorities.

When researching several issues or related claims, consider them one at a time. In this instance, you may have several lists of primary authorities, one for each claim you are researching. You may want to create a different binder for each claim.

B. Keeping Notes and Documents Online

The newest generation of online search tools—Lexis Advance and WestlawNext—allow you to keep track of your research and take notes online. While these tools serve experienced researchers well, new researchers are encouraged to use them in tandem with keeping notes as discussed above.

On Lexis Advance, a link at the top of every page leads to "My Workspace." Here you can "Create new folder" in the left margin. Your folders can be just for you, or you can create "Shared folders" for working with others. You can save into a folder documents, portions of documents, or searches. By highlighting text in documents, you will be able to copy the selected text to a folder, create an annotation for that text, or mark the text in color. Also available from "My Workspace" is a "History" link, which saves searches, search terms, documents you viewed, and deliveries for ninety days. You can search through your history by date, document type, or client.

WestlawNext provides a similar system of folders for your various research projects. Click on "Folders" at the top right corner of any screen, then click "New" in the left margin. As you conduct your research, you can add documents to the folders. The documents stay in your folders for as long as you remain a subscriber to WestlawNext. You may highlight and annotate the documents you place in your folders. In addition, WestlawNext provides a "History" link that saves all of your searches for a year. Filters allow you to view your searches by date, by terms, by the client whose problem you were researching (using a client identifier you assigned), and by the research event (i.e., whether you viewed a document, conducted a search, or used KeyCite).

III. Organizing Analysis

In addition to taking notes that summarize the research process with one of the methods discussed above, keep notes that summarize your analytical progress. Analytical notes provide a basis for organizing your arguments and writing your document. These notes do not have to be formal or typed; you are likely the only person who will read them. The notes should be written in your own words, not cut and pasted from the authorities you find. Simply cutting and pasting text is easy because it requires little real thinking. In contrast, deciding what is important enough to include in notes and expressing those ideas in your own words will increase your understanding of the legal issues involved.

As you find sources that are not relevant, or that duplicate information better provided by another source, make a few notes on your list of authorities. If a source is not relevant, strike through it on the list. You can use the "reviewing" or "commenting" toolbar to strike through irrelevant authorities, or you can move them to a separate document. Do not completely delete references to irrelevant authorities or you may later find yourself accidentally reading them again.

Secondary sources. Write a one-page summary for each secondary source you consult. Begin the summary with the title, author, and other citation information for the source. In your own words, summarize the relevant analysis in the source, including references to specific pages. Try to include a few sentences explaining how this source relates to your research.

Enacted law. Because the exact words of constitutions, statutes, and regulations are so important, you should print or photocopy the text of these provisions. Then, to fully understand a complex provision, you should outline it. Highlighting is sufficient only if the text is very short and clear. Be sure to refer to the definition sections of statutes; where important terms are not defined, make a note to look for judicial definitions. Also be sure to read statutes that are cross-referenced in any pertinent statute. Check statutory annotations for cross-references to relevant regulations.

Cases. Brief all relevant cases by explaining their key components in your own words. Be sure you understand the procedural posture and the standard of review applied in each case. Also be sure that you understand the facts of cases. Drawing a timeline or a chart of the relationships between the parties may be helpful. Concentrate your effort on the court's reasoning; too many briefs created by novices focus on facts or general rules, without paying sufficient attention to how the court applied those rules to the specific situation before it. Include the full citation in your brief, and note the pages that points in your brief come from (i.e., include the pinpoint pages that you will have to cite in a written document). Summarize your thoughts on the case: How do you anticipate using this case in your analysis? Which element does it address? Does it resolve certain issues for your problem? Does it raise new questions?

Updating. When you first look at a source online, note its Shepard's or KeyCite symbol. If the symbol is negative, stop to determine whether the source is still good law before basing your analysis on it. Later, carefully update each authority you use in developing your argument. Consider using an "Alert" function in the citator to keep you posted on any changes as you work on your project. If you need to expand your list of authorities, use updating not only to validate sources but also as a research tool.

Outlining. Because the most effective research often occurs in conjunction with the careful analysis of your particular project, try to develop an outline of your client's legal problem as soon as you can. An initial outline may be based on issues listed in a secondary source, the requirements of a statute, or the elements of a common law claim. If outlining feels too restrictive, consider using a flow chart, index cards, or an analysis box. An analysis box is simply a chart that organizes authorities by issue or element; a sample is shown in Table 11-3, following a description of the client's problem earlier in the chapter. The outline or chart should enable you to synthesize the law, apply the law to your client's facts, and reach a conclusion on the desired outcome.

IV. Ending Research

One of the most difficult parts of legal research is knowing when to stop researching. In practice, court deadlines or a supervisor's timeline will limit the number of hours you spend on a research

Table 11-3. Sample Analysis Chart

<u>Research Question</u>: Can a client recover against the driver of a car when he heard but did not see the accident that injured his wife?

Issue	Authority	Case Summary	Client Facts	Conclusion
1. Were client and victim "closely related"?	*Thing*	plaintiff must be a relative living in the same house or a parent, sibling, child, or grand-parent of the victim	injured party was client's wife	client was closely re-lated to the victim
2. Was client "present" at the scene and "then aware" of the injury?	*Wilks*	plaintiff must be instantly aware of likely severe injury; was in different room of house when vacuum exploded; met this element	client heard car crash as it happened; was in the adjacent restaurant	client was present be-cause he was close to the crash scene where he had just left his wife and he knew about the crash as it was hap-pening
	Air Crash	plaintiff watched house burn knowing family was inside because she'd left minutes before; met this element	client had left his wife at the table moments before	
	Thing	plaintiff was nearby when car crash occurred but wasn't aware of it at the time; did not meet this element	client heard crash, saw umbrella fall, and felt mirror pieces	

project. If research costs are going to be passed along to the client, the client's willingness and ability to pay are also considerations.

In the rare situation without external constraints, you can be confident ending your research in the following instances: First, you might find an authority that answers the client's legal question clearly and definitively. Alternatively, when your research in various sources leads back to the same authorities, you can be confident that you have been thorough and stop.

If you do not find an answer or if your research does not begin circling back to the same authorities, ending research might feel premature, but you cannot search forever. Review your analytical outline and see whether each point has sufficient support from primary authority in your jurisdiction. If not, look for persuasive authority, either from another jurisdiction or from a respected secondary source. As a final check on your thoroughness, go through each step of the basic research process to ensure you considered each one in your own research strategy for this particular project.

If you have found nothing, it may be that nothing exists. Before reaching that conclusion, expand your research terms and look in a few more secondary sources. Consider whether other jurisdictions may have helpful persuasive authority. It may be that you have encountered a new legal issue where you will get to help formulate the law as you assist your client.

Chapter 12

Legal Citation

Lawyers use legal citations to prove that arguments in legal documents are well researched and that analysis is well supported. Legal citations tell the reader where to find the authorities relied on and indicate the level of analytical support the authorities provide.[1] Because citation information is given in abbreviated form, using a uniform and widely recognized format ensures that the reader will understand the information being conveyed.

This chapter addresses the formats used to convey citation information. The *California Style Manual* (*CSM*)[2] will be explained first. This is the citation manual used by California state courts. Then the chapter will turn to the two national citation manuals, the *ALWD Citation Manual: A Professional System of Citation*[3] and *The Bluebook: A Uniform System of Citation*.[4] A lawyer writing to a state court in

---

1. In practice documents like office memoranda and court briefs, legal citations are typically included in the text of legal documents rather than being placed in footnotes or listed in a bibliography.

2. Edward W. Jessen, *California Style Manual* (4th ed., West 2000) ("*CSM*") (sometimes referred to as the "gold book" or the "orange book"). In this chapter, footnote references to the *CSM* will be to rule numbers (e.g., *CSM* § 1:2[A]).

3. ALWD & Darby Dickerson, *ALWD Citation Manual* (4th ed., Aspen Publishers 2010) ("*ALWD Manual*"). In this chapter, footnote references to the *ALWD Manual* provide the rule number in this format: *ALWD* Rule 12.12(a).

4. *The Bluebook: A Uniform System of Citation* (The Columbia Law Review et al. eds., 19th ed., The Harvard Law Review Ass'n 2010) ("*Bluebook*"). In this chapter, footnote references to the *Bluebook* include the rule number in this format: *Bluebook* Rule 18.1.

California has the option of using either the *California Style Manual* or the *Bluebook*, but a single style of citation must be used throughout the document.[5]

The *CSM*, the *ALWD Manual*, and the *Bluebook* are reference manuals. The key to good citation format is to learn the general structure of the manual used in your office and to know how to use it, not to read all three manuals cover-to-cover or try to memorize the rules.

I. The *California Style Manual*

A. Orientation to the *CSM*

The first three chapters of the *California Style Manual* cover citations for cases; constitutions, statutes, and rules; and secondary sources. The fourth chapter addresses matters of style (capitalization, quotations, numbers, italics, and punctuation). The final two chapters explain the editorial policies of the official reporters for California cases and case titles.

The *CSM* includes both a table of contents and an index. Both are helpful for finding relevant rules. In addition, each of the six chapters contains a more detailed table of contents. A "Table of Frequently Used Abbreviations" appears at the front of the book, but most of the information is repeated in relevant rules. Those rule-specific lists are often more helpful because similar material can be reviewed quickly. Thus, looking at the list of state and reporter abbreviations in § 1:30 will be easier than looking for each state and reporter in the table in the front of the book.

Following the rules in the *CSM* results in citations that look a bit different from the citations used in other states or in the national citation manuals. Among the most obvious differences are (1) placement of the entire citation in parentheses, (2) the location of the date immediately after the name of the case, and (3) the use of *supra* in short citations. Even with these cosmetic differences, citations under

---

5. Cal. R. Ct. Rule 1.200.

all three citation manuals convey the same essential information. Indeed, the *CSM* relies on the *Bluebook* to fill in any gaps.[6] Examples of *CSM* citations are given in Table 12-1. Brief explanations for case and statutory citations follow.

Table 12-1. Example Citations from the *California Style Manual*

State Constitution	Cal. Const., art. VI, § 10.
State Statute	Code Civ. Pro. § 340.5.
State Case	*People v. Davis* (1998) 18 Cal.4th 712.
State Rule	Cal. Code Regs., tit. 14, § 916.2.
Law Review Article	Lessig, *The Zones of Cyberspace* (1996) 48 Stan. L.Rev. 1403.

B. Case Citations under the *CSM*

1. Full Citations to Cases

A full citation to a case includes (1) the name of the case, (2) the date the case was decided, (3) the court that decided the case, (4) the volume and abbreviation of the official reporter in which the case was published, (5) the first page of the case, (6) the exact page in the case that contains the idea being cited,[7] and (7) parallel citations, if there are any.[8] Remember that, despite the online availability of cases, citations still reference the print volumes.

> EXAMPLES: (*Brown v. Bd. of Educ.* (1955) 349 U.S. 294, 300 [75 S.Ct. 753, 99 L.Ed. 1083].)

---

6. *See e.g. CSM* §§ 1:35, 1:36.

7. This page is commonly called the *pinpoint* cite, *pincite*, or *jump* cite, though the *CSM* uses the term *point* cite. *CSM* § 1:1[E].

8. *CSM* § 1:1.

(*People v. Davis* (1998) 18 Cal.4th 712, 718
[76 Cal.Rptr.2d 770, 958 P.2d 1083].)

(*Flint v. Dennison* (9th Cir. 2007) 488 F.3d 816.)

Use the shortened name of the case from the running head of a print reporter or the shortened name shown in an online source.[9] Words that appear in the table of abbreviations at the front of the *CSM* may be abbreviated; other abbreviations are left to the writer's discretion. See Table 12-5 later in this chapter for a few *CSM* abbreviations, compared to abbreviations used in the national manuals. Between the parties' names, place a lower case "v" followed by a period. Italicize the parties' names and the "v."[10]

Next, in a parenthetical, give the court that decided the case and the jurisdiction, unless both will be clear from the reporter abbreviation.[11] For instance, only decisions of the California Supreme Court are reported in *California Reports*, so citations to that reporter can omit the court and jurisdiction in the parenthetical. Then, in the same parenthetical, give the year the decision was filed.[12]

Following the parenthetical, provide the volume and abbreviation to the relevant print reporter.[13] Abbreviations for California, regional, and federal reporters are included in the table of abbreviations. In addition, abbreviations for California reporters are given in §§ 1:13 through 1:16, abbreviations for regional reporters are listed in § 1:30, and abbreviations for federal reporters are given in §§ 1:32[A], 1:33[A], and 1:34[A]. Pay special attention to the series of the reporter, as many reporters are no longer in a first series. Note that no spaces appear between abbreviations of reporter titles (i.e., there's no space between Cal. and 4th). In the *Davis* example above, 18 is the volume number and Cal.4th is the reporter abbreviation for

---

9. *CSM* § 1:1[A].
10. *CSM* § 1:1[B].
11. *CSM* § 1:1[D].
12. *Id.*
13. *CSM* § 1:1[E].

California Reports, Fourth Series. The reporters used for California appellate case citations are summarized in Table 12-2.

**Table 12-2. *CSM* Reporter Abbreviations for
California Appellate Cases**

Reporter	California Decisions Reported	Abbreviations
California Reports	Supreme Court	Cal., Cal.2d, Cal.3d, Cal.4th
California Appellate Reports	Court of Appeal	Cal.App., Cal.App.2d, Cal.App.3d, Cal.App.4th
West's California Reporter	Supreme Court Court of Appeal from 1959	Cal.Rptr., Cal.Rptr.2d, Cal.Rptr.3d
Pacific Reporter	Supreme Court Court of Appeal through 1959	P., P.2d, P.3d

After the reporter abbreviation, include both the first page of the case and the page containing the idea that you are referencing, separated by a comma and a space.[14] The first page of the *Davis* case in the earlier example is 712, and the page containing the specific idea being cited is 718.[15]

In brackets following this required information, you may provide parallel citations.[16] You can also note significant subsequent history.[17]

---

14. *Id.*

15. When using an online version of a case, remember that a reference to a specific reporter page may change in the middle of a computer screen or a printed page. Thus, the page number indicated at the top of the screen or printed page may not be the page where the relevant information is located. For example, if the notation *719 appeared in the text before the relevant information, the pinpoint cite would be to page 719, not page 718.

16. *CSM* § 1:1[F]. Including parallel citations is considered better practice. *CSM* § 1:12.

17. *CSM* § 1:11.

The citation information above, based on the location of a case in a print reporter, is preferred. If the case is too recent to have been published in a print reporter, or if the case will only be available online, cite it using the name of parties, court, full date on which the opinion was filed, the court's docket number,[18] and the online citation in brackets. For example, until the following case was available in *California Reports*, it could have been cited to Westlaw: (*People v. Anzalone* (Apr. 15, 2013, S192536) __ Cal. 4th __ [2013 WL 1501573].) Other online citation sources include Lexis, the California Daily Opinion Service (abbreviated C.D.O.S.), and the URL on the particular court's website. The bracketed citation to Westlaw or other online sources is helpful, but not required.

2. Short Citations to Cases

After a full citation has been used once to introduce an authority, short citations are subsequently used to cite to the same authority. If a case will be cited frequently, a shortened version of the case name can be used after the full citation. This shortened version may be simply the name of the first party listed.[19]

Within the same paragraph, use *ibid.* to cite the identical page in the case. Use *id.* followed by "at p." and the page number to refer to a different page of the same case. Note that *ibid.* and *id.* can be used only to refer to a case already cited in the same paragraph and only if no other citations have intervened.

> EXAMPLE: In *People v. Davis* (1998) 18 Cal.4th 712, 714, the defendant argued for reversal of a burglary conviction. The defendant had placed a forged check in a chute at a check-cashing business's walk-up facility. (*Ibid.*) After an extensive review of the crime of burglary in California, the Supreme Court agreed that no burglary had taken place. (*Id.* at p. 724.)

---

18. Docket numbers are explained in *CSM* § 1:17[B].
19. *CSM* § 1:1[C].

To cite a case in a later paragraph (or in the same paragraph after an intervening citation), use the case name, *supra*, the reporter volume and abbreviation, and the relevant pinpoint page numbers.

EXAMPLE: (*Davis, supra*, 18 Cal.4th at p. 715.)

3. Signals

A citation must show the level of support each authority provides. Introductory signals show this support. Note that the strongest support is shown by using no signal. The more common signals are explained in Table 12-3.[20]

Table 12-3. *CSM* **Introductory Signals**

No signal	•	The source cited provides direct support for the idea in the sentence.
	•	The citation identifies the source of a quotation.
See	•	The source cited offers indirect support for the idea in the sentence.
	•	The source cited offers support in dicta.
	•	The source cited offers support in a concurring or dissenting opinion.
See also	•	The source cited provides additional support for the idea in the sentence.
	•	The support offered by *see also* is indirect.
E.g.	•	The source cited is representative of other authorities that support the idea explained in the sentence.

4. Explanatory Parentheticals

After a citation, a short parenthetical can help show the relationship between the cited authority and the idea in the text.[21] The most

---

20. *CSM* § 1:4.
21. *CSM* § 1:6.

effective parentheticals are very brief descriptions of the facts or holding of the case or short quotes. Complete sentences are disfavored in parentheticals.

> EXAMPLE: The California Supreme Court has stated in dicta that inserting a hand into a library chute to steal books would constitute burglary. (*See People v. Davis* (1998) 18 Cal.4th 712, 723 [holding that passing a forged check through a chute at a check-cashing business was not burglary]).

C. Statutory Citations under the *CSM*

A citation to a California statute requires both the abbreviated name of the code[22] and the section number.[23] Code abbreviations are listed in §2:8. To show a subdivision of a particular statutory section, use the abbreviation "subd."

A citation to a federal statute includes the title number, code abbreviation, and section number. Subdivisions are shown by enclosing the letter in parentheses. While citation to the official *United States Code* (U.S.C.) is preferred, citation to either *United States Code Annotated* (U.S.C.A.) or *United States Code Service* (U.S.C.S.) is acceptable under the *CSM*. Note that federal statutes do not have code names like California statutes have. Note also that a statutory citation includes neither a publisher nor a date.

> EXAMPLES: (Code Civ. Proc., §564, subd. (a).)
>
>   (28 U.S.C. §1441(a).)

D. Quotations

The *CSM* provides clear instruction on quotations: "Quoted material should correspond exactly with its original source in wording, spelling, capitalization, internal punctuation, and citation style."[24] All

---

22. *CSM* §2:8.
23. *CSM* §2:5[A], 2:6.
24. *CSM* §4:27.

modifications, additions, or deletions must be shown. The rules for quoted material are provided in *CSM* § 4:12 through § 4:27.

II. National Citation Manuals

The two most widely used national citation manuals are the *ALWD Citation Manual* and the *Bluebook*. Both are large booklets that contain hundreds of pages of citation rules, examples, and explanations.

The *ALWD Manual* is considered by many the best citation manual for novices and for practitioners because it uses a single system of citation for legal memoranda, court documents, law review articles, and all other legal documents. The explanations are clear, and the examples are given in the format required in the memoranda and briefs attorneys write.

The *Bluebook* is the oldest, most widely known citation manual. The difficulty with this manual is that it contains two different citation formats: one for law review footnotes and another for practice documents. Most of the *Bluebook*'s explanations and examples are relevant to law review footnotes, which use different fonts (e.g., italics, large and small capitals) than those used in citations in practice documents. Even so, the *Bluebook* is so well known that most attorneys use the term "Bluebooking" to mean checking citations for consistent format.

Under the current editions (4th for the *ALWD Manual* and 19th for the *Bluebook*) citations for practitioner documents are virtually identical. Anticipated changes in the 5th edition of the *ALWD Manual* should result in completely identical citations.

A. Navigating the *ALWD Manual* and the *Bluebook*

1. Index

The index at the back of each manual is quite extensive, and in most instances it is more helpful than the table of contents. Most often, you should begin working with a citation manual by referring to the index.

2. *"Fast Formats" and "Quick Reference"*

Many chapters of the *ALWD Citation Manual* begin with citation examples, in tables called "Fast Formats." A list of these "Fast Formats" is provided on the inside front cover of the *ALWD Manual*.

The *Bluebook* contains two "Quick Reference" guides. The one on the inside front cover provides sample citations for law review footnotes. The guide on the inside back cover gives example citations for court documents and legal memoranda. Be sure to consult the appropriate guide for your writing task because the citations differ from one another.

3. *Bluebook* "Bluepages"

The *Bluebook* opens with a section devoted to citations for practitioners. These Bluepages provide information for and additional examples of citations used in documents other than law review articles.[25] When using the *Bluebook*, remember that only the Bluepages and the reference guide at the back of the manual provide examples for practice documents. Thus, a student or lawyer using the *Bluebook* must use the Bluepages to translate examples in the rest of the manual from law review format into the format used in practice documents.

---

25. The Bluepages are helpful in knowing which font to use in practice document citations. The Bluepages list the following items that should be italicized or underlined in citations in legal memoranda and court documents: case names, titles of books and articles, and introductory signals. Items not included in the list should appear in regular type. Remember to follow the typeface instructions in the Bluepages even when other *Bluebook* examples include large and small capital letters.

4. ALWD *Appendices and* Bluebook *Tables*

The back section of each citation manual contains lists of abbreviations and other helpful information. In the *ALWD Manual* these are called "appendices."[26] Pages with dark blue edges at the back of the *Bluebook* contain "tables" with similar information.[27]

B. Citing California Material

Because these manuals are designed for national use, their citations for California material vary from California practice. A summary of abbreviations for California material appears in Appendix 1 of the *ALWD Manual* and in Table T1.3 of the *Bluebook*. Examples for citations in briefs and memoranda are included in Table 12-4 in this chapter. Compare these examples to the California citations shown in Table 12-1.

C. Case Citations

As with the *California Style Manual*, case citations under *ALWD* and *Bluebook* rules are most often to print reporters.

1. *Full Citations to Cases*

In both *ALWD* and *Bluebook* format, a full citation to a case includes (1) the name of the case, (2) the volume and reporter in which the case is published, (3) the first page of the case, (4) the exact page in the case that contains the idea you are citing (i.e., the *pinpoint* or *jump* cite), (5) the court that decided the case, and (6) the year the

---

26. Especially helpful *ALWD Manual* appendices are Appendix 1 (federal and state sources); Appendix 3 (months, case names); Appendix 4 (courts); Appendix 5 (periodicals); and Appendix 6 (sample memorandum).

27. Especially helpful *Bluebook* tables are Table T1.1 (federal sources); Table T1.3 (state sources); Table T6 (case names); Table T12 (months); and Table T13 (periodicals).

Table 12-4. Example California Citations in
ALWD and *Bluebook* Format

Type of Document	*ALWD* Format	*Bluebook* Format
State Constitution	Cal. Const., art. VI, § 10.	Cal. Const., art. VI, § 10.
State Statute	Cal. Civ. Proc. Code Ann. § 340.5 (West 2006).	Cal. Civ. Proc. Code. § 340.5 (West 2006).
State Case	*People v. Davis*, 18 Cal. 4th 712, 714 (1998).	*People v. Davis*, 18 Cal. 4th 712, 714 (1998).
State Regulation	Cal. Code Regs., tit. 14, § 916.2 (2013).	Cal. Code Regs., tit. 14, § 916.2 (2013).
Law Review Article	Lawrence Lessig, *The Zones of Cyberspace*, 48 Stan. L. Rev. 1403 (1996).	Lawrence Lessig, *The Zones of Cyberspace*, 48 Stan. L. Rev. 1403 (1996).

case was decided.[28] The key points for citation to cases are given below, along with examples.

Include the name of just the first party on each side, even if several are listed in the case caption. If the party is an individual, include only the party's last name. If the party is a business or organization, shorten the party's name by using abbreviations provided in the citation manual you are using.[29] The *Bluebook*'s abbreviations list is much shorter than the list in the *ALWD Manual*. While the *CSM* abbreviates fewer words than either national manual, its style more often follows that of the *ALWD Manual*. In some instances, the *ALWD Manual* provides two options for abbreviations; be sure to use the same abbreviation consistently throughout your document. See Table 12-5 in this section for a comparison of abbreviations from the three manuals. Note that in the *Bluebook*, "United States" is never abbreviated when it is a party's name.[30]

---

28. *ALWD* Rule 12; *Bluebook* Rule B4.
29. *ALWD* Appendix 3; *Bluebook* Table T6.
30. *Bluebook* Rule 10.2.2.

Table 12-5. Comparison of Selected Abbreviations in *CSM*, *ALWD*, and *Bluebook* Formats

Word	*CSM*	*ALWD* (Appendix 3)	*Bluebook* (Table T6)
Associate	*	Assoc.	Assoc.
Association	Assn.	Assn. or Ass'n	Ass'n
Center	*	Ctr.	Ctr.
Central	*	C.	Cent.
Community	*	*	Cmty.
Department	Dept.	Dept. or Dep't	Dep't
Lawyer	Law.	Law.	*
National	Nat.	Natl. or Nat'l	Nat'l
Partnership	*	Partn. or P'ship	P'ship
Resource[s]	*	*	Res.
University	U. or Univ.	U.	Univ.

* The three manuals do not abbreviate all the same words.

Between the parties' names, place a lower case "v" followed by a period. The parties' names and the "v" may be italicized or underlined. Use the style preferred by your office consistently throughout each document.[31] Do not combine italics and underlining in one cite or within a single document. Place a comma after the second party's name, but do not italicize or underline this comma.

EXAMPLES: *Flint v. Dennison*, 488 F.3d 816, 820 (9th Cir. 2007).

Flint v. Dennison, 488 F.3d 816, 820 (9th Cir. 2007).

Next, give the volume and the abbreviation for the reporter in which the case is found.[32] Always note carefully whether the reporter

---

31. *ALWD* Rule 12.2(a) (case names) and Rule 1.1 (typeface choice); *Bluebook* Rule B1.

32. For cases available only on Lexis or Westlaw, follow *ALWD* Rule 12.12(a) and *Bluebook* Rule B4.1.4 and Rule 18.3.1.

is in its first, second, third, or fourth series.[33] In the *Flint* example above, 488 is the volume number and F.3d is the reporter abbreviation for *Federal Reporter, Third Series.*

Following the reporter name, include both the first page of the case and the pinpoint page containing the idea that you are referencing, separated by a comma and a space.[34] The first page of the *Flint* case above is 816, and the page containing the specific idea being cited is 820. If the pinpoint page you are citing is also the first page of the case, then the same page number will appear twice.[35]

In a parenthetical after this information, indicate the court that decided the case.[36] In Appendix 1 of the *ALWD Manual* and in Table T1 of the *Bluebook*, the notations for the courts of each jurisdiction are included in parentheses just after the name of the court. In the *Flint* example, the Ninth Circuit Court of Appeals, a federal court, decided the case.

When the reporter abbreviation clearly indicates which court decided a case, do not repeat that information in the parenthetical. For example, only cases of the United States Supreme Court are reported in *United States Reports*, abbreviated U.S. Repeating the court notation (U.S.) in citations to that reporter would be duplicative. In contrast, *Pacific Reporter, Third Series*, abbreviated P.3d, publishes decisions from courts within several states, so the court that decided a particular case needs to be indicated parenthetically. In the second example below, "Cal." indicates that the decision came from the California Supreme Court rather than from another court whose decisions are also published in the *Pacific Reporter*.

---

33. Abbreviations for common reporters are found in Chart 12.1 of the *ALWD Manual*; abbreviations for reporters for California cases are included in Appendix I. The *Bluebook* does not have a comprehensive list of common reporters; check Table T1 for reporters in a particular jurisdiction.

34. *ALWD* Rule 5 and Rule 12.5; *Bluebook* Rule B4.1.2.

35. When using an online version of a case, remember that a reference to a specific reporter page may change in the middle of a computer screen or a printed page. *See* note 15 *supra.*

36. *ALWD* Rule 12.6(a); *Bluebook* Rule B4.1.3.

EXAMPLES: *Brown v. Bd. of Educ.*, 349 U.S. 294, 300 (1955).

Ketchum v. Moses, 17 P.3d 735, 736 (Cal. 2001).

Because *West's California Reporter* publishes cases from both the California Supreme Court and the California Courts of Appeal, all citations to that reporter have to include the court designation in the parenthetical.

When citing to Court of Appeal cases published in *West's California Reporter*, the *ALWD Manual* requires that the district be included,[37] whereas the *Bluebook* says not to include that information.[38] In practice, you could drop the "App." in the *ALWD* cite, as it is widely known that the districts are part of the Court of Appeal.

ALWD EXAMPLE: *People v. Wise*, 30 Cal. Rptr. 2d 413 (App. 1st Dist. 1994).

BLUEBOOK EXAMPLE: *People v. Wise*, 30 Cal. Rptr. 2d 413 (Ct. App. 1994).

The last piece of required information in most cites is the date the case was decided. For cases published in reporters, give only the year of decision,[39] not the month or day.[40]

Prior and subsequent history can be added to the end of a citation, as shown in the example below.[41]

EXAMPLE: The only time that the Supreme Court addressed the requirement of motive for an EMTALA claim, the court rejected that requirement. *Roberts v. Galen of Va.*, 525 U.S. 249, 253 (1999), *rev'g* 111 F.3d 405 (6th Cir. 1997).

---

37. *ALWD* Rule 12.6(b)(2).

38. *Bluebook* Rule 10.4(a).

39. *ALWD* Rule 12.7; *Bluebook* Rule B4.1.3 and Rule 10.5.

40. For cases available only online, give the month abbreviation, date, and year. *ALWD* Rule 12.12(a); *Bluebook* Rule B4.1.4, and Rule 18.3.1.

41. *ALWD* Rules 12.8–12.10; *Bluebook* Rule B4.1.6.

2. Short Citations to Cases

After giving the full citation to introduce an authority, use short citations to cite to the same authority.[42] When the immediately preceding cite is to the same source and the same page, use *id.* as the short cite. When the second cite is to a different page within the same source, follow the *id.* with "at" and the new pinpoint page number. Capitalize *id.* when it begins a citation sentence, just as the beginning of any sentence is capitalized.[43]

If the cite is from a previously cited case that is not the immediately preceding cite, give the name of one of the parties (generally the first party named in the full cite), the volume, the reporter, and the pinpoint page following "at."[44] The format "*Davis* at 714," consisting of just a case name and page number, is incorrect. The volume and reporter abbreviation are also needed.

> EXAMPLE: In *People v. Davis*, 18 Cal. 4th 712, 714 (1998), the defendant argued for reversal of a burglary conviction. The defendant had placed a forged check in a chute at a check-cashing business's walk-up facility. *Id.* After an extensive review of the crime of burglary in California, the Supreme Court disapproved *People v. Ravenscroft*, 198 Cal. App. 3d 639 (1988), on which the prosecution had relied, and agreed that no burglary had taken place. *Davis*, 18 Cal. 4th at 724.

The example above shows short citations under *Bluebook* and *ALWD* style, not *CMS* format. Note that under the current *ALWD Manual* the *Ravenscroft* citation in the example would include "2d Dist." in the parenthetical with the date. The next edition of the *ALWD Manual* is expected to omit that information.

---

42. *ALWD* Rules 11.2 and 11.3; *Bluebook* Rule B4.2.
43. *ALWD* Rule 11.3(d); *Bluebook* Rule B4.2.
44. *ALWD* Rule 12.20; *Bluebook* Rule B4.2.

D. Federal Statutory Citations

Cite federal laws to the *United States Code* (U.S.C.), the official code for federal statutes, when that series contains the current statutory language.[45] Because that series is published so slowly, however, the current language will most likely be found in a commercial version, either *United States Code Annotated* (U.S.C.A., published by West) or *United States Code Service* (U.S.C.S., published by Lexis-Nexis).

The citation to a federal statute includes the title number, code abbreviation, section number, publisher (except for U.S.C.), and date. The date given in statutory cites is the date of the volume in which the statute is published, not the date the statute was enacted. If the language appears only in the pocket part, include only the date of the pocket part.[46] If the language of only a portion of the statute is reprinted in the pocket part, include the dates of both the bound volume and the pocket part.[47]

> EXAMPLE: 43 U.S.C.A. § 1786 (West Supp. 2012).
> (Statutory language appears in the
> supplemental pocket part only)

> EXAMPLE: 43 U.S.C.A. § 1543 (West 2007 & Supp. 2012).
> (Statutory language appears in both the
> bound volume and the supplemental pocket
> part)

The *ALWD Manual* is more permissive than the *Bluebook* about citing online versions of the code. When citing an online version, include in the date parenthetical both the name of the online source (e.g., Westlaw) and how current the source is.[48]

---

45. *ALWD* Rule 14; *Bluebook* Rule B5.1.1.
46. *ALWD* Rule 8.1; *Bluebook* Rule 3.1.
47. *ALWD* Rule 14.2(f); *Bluebook* Rule 12.2.2.
48. *ALWD* Rule 14.5.

E. Signals

As noted in the discussion of *CSM,* introductory signals show the type of support each authority provides. The more common signals are explained in Table 12-3.[49]

F. Explanatory Parentheticals

Similar to parentheticals under the *CSM,* both the *ALWD Manual* and the *Bluebook* provide for explanatory parentheticals following citations.[50] Sometimes this parenthetical information conveys to the reader the weight of the authority (e.g., a case may have been decided *en banc* or *per curiam*). Or the case may have been decided by a narrow split among the judges who heard the case. Parenthetical information might also provide the names of judges who joined in a dissenting, concurring, or plurality opinion.[51]

> EXAMPLE: Excluding relevant evidence during a sentencing hearing may deny the criminal defendant due process. *Green v. Georgia,* 442 U.S. 95, 97 (1979) (per curiam) (regarding testimony of co-defendant's confession in rape and murder case).

Because readers tend to skim citations, and especially parentheticals within citations, be careful not to hide a critical part of the court's analysis in a parenthetical at the end of a long citation.

G. Quotations

In every citation system, the words, punctuation, and capitalization of a quote must appear exactly as they are in the original.[52] Any alter-

---

49. *ALWD* Rule 44; *Bluebook* Rule B3.
50. *ALWD* Rule 46; *Bluebook* Rule B4.1.5 and Rule B11.
51. *ALWD* Rule 12.11; *Bluebook* Rule B4.1.5.
52. *ALWD* Rules 47, 48, and 49; *Bluebook,* Rule 5. There is one slight difference in the quotation rules: For the *Bluebook,* quotations that have fifty or more words must be set off in indented blocks. *Bluebook* Rule 5.1. That means the writer must count words to know how many words the quotation

ations or omissions must be indicated. Include commas and periods inside quotation marks; place other punctuation outside the quotation marks unless it is included in the original text. Also, try to provide smooth transitions between your text and the quoted text.

H. Additional Citation Details

The following citation details are second nature to users of the national manuals, though they frequently trip up both students and practitioners familiar with a particular state's citation rules.

- *Numbers.* It is most common in legal documents to spell out numbers zero through ninety-nine and to use numerals for larger numbers. However, always spell out a number that is the first word of a sentence.[53]

- *Ordinal abbreviations.* The most confusing are 2d for "Second" and 3d for "Third" because they differ from the common non-legal formats 2nd and 3rd.[54]

- *Spacing of abbreviations.* Do not insert a space between abbreviations of single capital letters. For example, there is no space in U.S. Moreover, ordinal numbers like 1st, 2d, and 3d are considered single capital letters for purposes of this rule. Thus, there is no space in P.2d or F.3d because 2d and 3d are considered single capital letters. Leave one space on each side of elements of an abbreviation that are not single capital letters. For example, F. Supp. 2d has a space on each side of "Supp."[55]

---

contains. In contrast, the *ALWD Manual* requires indented blocks for quotes that are fifty or more words *or* quotes that span four or more lines of typed text. *ALWD* Rule 47.5(a).

53. *ALWD* Rule 4.2; *Bluebook* Rule 6.2(a).

54. *ALWD* Rule 4.3; *Bluebook* Rule 6.2(b).

55. *ALWD* Rule 2.2; *Bluebook* Rule 6.1.

III. *Bluebook* Citations for Law Review Articles

While the rules discussed above also apply to citations in footnotes to law review articles following the *Bluebook*, that manual uses different fonts — including large and small capital letters — for law review footnote citations. The example in Table 12-6 shows a statutory citation using the *ALWD Manual*, the *Bluebook* format for legal memoranda and court documents, and the *Bluebook* format for law review footnotes.

Table 12-6. Comparison of *ALWD* and *Bluebook* Formats

ALWD Manual All Documents	*Bluebook*	
	Legal Memoranda	Law Review Articles
Cal. Penal Code Ann. §451 (West 2010).	Cal. Penal Code §451 (West 2010).	Cal. Penal Code §451 (West 2010).

Using the *Bluebook* to write citations for law review articles is considerably easier than using it for practice documents because almost all of the examples given in the *Bluebook* are in law review format. Table 12-7 of this chapter summarizes the typeface used for several common sources and gives examples.

Law review articles place citations in footnotes or endnotes, instead of placing citations in the main text of the document.[56] Most law review footnotes include text in ordinary type, in italics, and in large and small capital letters.[57] This convention is not universal, and each law review selects the typefaces it will use. Some law reviews may use only ordinary type and italics. Others may use just ordinary type.[58] Assuming you are submitting an article to a law review that uses all three typefaces, *Bluebook* Rule 2 dictates which typeface to use for each type of authority.

---

56. *Bluebook* Rule 1.1(a).
57. *Bluebook* Rule 2.2(a).
58. *Bluebook* Rule 2.1.

Table 12-7. *Bluebook* Typeface for Law Review Footnotes

Item	Type used	Example
Cases	Use ordinary type for case names in full citations. (See text for further explanation.)	Legal Servs. Corp. v. Velazquez, 531 U.S. 533 (2001).
Books	Use large and small capital letters for the author and the title.	DAVID S. ROMANTZ & KATHLEEN ELLIOTT VINSON, LEGAL ANALYSIS: THE FUNDAMENTAL SKILL (2d. ed 2009).
Periodical articles	Use ordinary type for the author's name, italics for the title, and large and small capitals for the periodical.	Linda Berger, *Lies Between Mommy and Daddy: The Case for Recognizing Spousal Emotional Distress Claims Based on Domestic Deceit that Interferes with Parent-Child Relationships*, 33 LOY. L.A. L. REV. 417 (2000).
Explanatory phrases	Use italics for all explanatory phrases, such as *aff'g, cert. denied, rev'd*, and *overruled by*.	Legal Servs. Corp. v. Velazquez, 531 U.S. 533 (2001), *aff'g* 164 F.3d 757 (2d Cir. 1999).
Introductory signals	Use italics for all introductory signals, such as *see* and *e.g.* when they appear in citations, as opposed to text.	*See id.*

The typeface used for a case name depends on (1) whether the case appears in the main text of the article or in a footnote and (2) how the case is used. When a case name appears in the main text of the article or in a textual sentence of a footnote, it is italicized. By contrast, if a footnote contains an embedded citation, the case name is written in ordinary type. Similarly, when a full cite is given in a footnote, the case name is written in ordinary type. But when a short cite is used in footnotes, the case name is italicized.

IV. Citations Not Covered by a Manual

As comprehensive as the *CSM*, the *ALWD Manual*, and the *Bluebook* are, they do not definitively answer every citation question. When you cannot find a specific rule to cover a source you need to cite, look for rules regarding analogous sources. In creating a citation, always be guided by the purpose of citation: to allow a reader to find a source and to understand the type and weight of support it provides.

About the Authors

Hether C. Macfarlane has directed two legal writing programs: Albany School of Law (of which she is a graduate) and Pacific McGeorge School of Law (2000–2009). She is now a Professor of Lawyering Skills and teaches in the Pacific McGeorge Global Lawyering Skills program. She practiced law at the Washington, DC, office of Hunton & Williams, specializing in environmental and administrative law.

Aimee Dudovitz is an Associate Clinical Professor of Law at Loyola Law School—Los Angeles. After receiving her J.D. from the University of California, Davis, School of Law, she clerked for the Honorable Harry Pregerson of the Ninth Circuit and for the Honorable Dean D. Pregerson of the Central District of California. She practiced law in Los Angeles for nine years, including with Irell & Manella LLP and Strumwasser & Woocher LLP.

Suzanne E. Rowe began her legal career clerking for the Honorable Rudi M. Brewster of the Southern District of California. She has taught legal research and writing at the University of San Diego School of Law, Florida State University College of Law, and the University of Oregon School of Law, where she is currently the James L. and Ilene R. Hershner Professor. She is a graduate of Columbia University School of Law.

Index